[redacted]

ALICE MALSENIOR WALKER

An Annotated Bibliography: 1968-1986

Meckler's Studies and Bibliographies on Black Americans

1. *Alice Malsenior Walker: An Annotated Bibliography: 1968-1986*
Louis H. Pratt and Darnell D. Pratt
ISBN 0-88736-156-0 CIP 1988

ALICE MALSENIOR WALKER
An Annotated Bibliography: 1968-1986

Louis H. Pratt
Darnell D. Pratt

Meckler

[redacted]

Library of Congress Cataloging-in-Publication Data

Pratt, Louis H.
Alice Malsenior Walker: an annotated bibliography, 1968-1986.

(Meckler's studies and bibliographies on Black Americans; 1)
Bibliography: p.
Includes index.
1. Walker, Alice, 1944- --Bibliography.
I. Pratt, Darnell D. II. Title. III. Series.
Z8947.42.P7 1988 016.813'54 87-34816
[PS3573.A425]
ISBN 0-88736-156-0 (alk. paper)

Meckler Corporation, 11 Ferry Lane West, Westport, CT 06880
Meckler Ltd., Grosvenor Gardens House, Grosvenor Gardens,
London SW1W 0BS

Printed on acid free paper.
Manufactured in the United States of America

[redacted]

For

Gertrude Pratt Johnson
Catherine Mack Cooper

and

Hattie Pearl Dixon (1906-1969)
Madeline Harrison Thomas (1921-1983)

in recognition of
their zeal and ardor
in cultivating their gardens
and the special influence
which they have had on our lives.

Contents

Chronology

1944	Alice Malsenior Walker born February 9 in Eatonton, Georgia to Minnie Lue and Willie Lee Walker.
1952	Involved in accident which left her permanently blind in one eye.
1961	Received full scholarship for handicapped students, because of her partial blindness, to attend Spelman College.
1963	Transferred to Sarah Lawrence College. Came under tutelage of Muriel Rukeyser.
1965	Awarded B. A. degree from Sarah Lawrence College.
1966-67	Received Charles Merrill Writing Fellowship and Bread Loaf Writers Conference Scholarship.
1967	Won first prize in *American Scholar* Essay Contest for "The Civil Rights Movement: What Good Was It?" Awarded MacDowell Colony Fellowship to begin writing *The Third Life of Grange Copeland*. Published first short story, "To Hell With Dying." Married Melvyn R. Leventhal, a civil rights lawyer, on March 17.
1967-68	Served as consultant to Black Studies Friends of the Children of Mississippi.
1968	Published *Once: Poems*.
1969	Awarded National Endowment for the Arts Grant to complete *The Third Life of Grange Copeland*. Daughter, Rebecca Grant, was born.
1970	Published *The Third Life of Grange Copeland*.
1970-71	Appointed Writer-In-Residence at Tougaloo College.
1971	Awarded Radcliffe Institute Fellowship.
1972	Received Doctor of Philosophy degree from Russell Sage College.
1972-73	Served as lecturer in writing and literature at Wellesley College. Appointed lecturer in literature at the University of Massachusetts.

1973	Published *In Love and Trouble: Stories of Black Women* and *Revolutionary Petunias and Other Poems*. *Revolutionary Petunias* was nominated for the National Book Award and won the Lillian Smith Award from the Southern Regional Council.
1974	Published *Langston Hughes, American Poet*. Received the Rosenthal Award from the National Institute of Arts and Letters for the short story collection, *In Love and Trouble*. Became contributing editor for *Ms.*
1976	Published *Meridian*. Divorced from Melvyn Leventhal.
1977	Appointed Associate Professor of English at Yale University.
1978	Received the Guggenheim Award.
1979	Published *Good Night, Willie Lee, I'll See You in the Morning: Poems*. Edited *I Love Myself When I am Laughing, and Then Again When I am Looking Mean and Impressive*, a Zora Neale Hurston Reader.
1981	Published *You Can't Keep A Good Woman Down: Stories*.
1982	Published *The Color Purple*, which was nominated for the National Book Critics Circle Award.
1982-83	Appointed Fannie Hurst Professor at Brandeis University (Fall) and Distinguished Writer at the University of California, Berkeley (Spring).
1983	Published *In Search of Our Mothers' Gardens: Womanist Prose*. Became the first Black woman to receive the Pulitzer Prize for fiction for *The Color Purple*, which appeared on the Bestsellers' List of the *New York Times* for over twenty-five weeks. Won the American Book Award (hardcover category) for *The Color Purple*. Awarded Doctor of Humane Letters, University of Massachusetts at Amherst.
1984	Published *Horses Make a Landscape Look More Beautiful*. Awarded the Jim Townsend Prize for *The Color Purple*.
1985	Served as consultant for production of movie, *The Color Purple*, directed by Steven Spielberg, based on Walker's novel of the same name. The screenplay was written by Menno Meyjes, and the musical score was composed by Quincy Jones.

1986 Received first prize among the O. Henry Awards for "Kindred Spirits." The Color Purple won the Best Picture Award from the National Board of Review and eleven Academy Award nominations: Best Actress, Best Supporting Actress (2), Best Picture of the Year, Best Original Score, Best Original Song, Best Screenplay Adaptation, Best Cinematography, Best Art Direction, Best Costume Designs, and Best Makeup.

Preface

During the summer of 1984, The Color Purple was listed as a required reading for students in AML 4275--The Afro-American Novel class at Florida A and M University. About half of the students had already read the novel, and the others were knowledgeable about Walker vis a vis her recent signal honor as the first Black woman to garner the prestigious Pulitzer Prize for fiction. Interest and enthusiasm ran high, though it was partly mitigated by the students' inability to find bibliographic references for secondary sources. It was out of this need that we began the simultaneous tasks of compiling and organizing these listings and searching for a publisher.

This bibliography presents descriptive rather than evaluative annotations which are intended as a guide for the reader or researcher intent on exploring Alice Walker's social and literary philosophies and analyzing the growing body of critical exposition and interpretation of her work. Thus, every effort has been made to list references which either present significant aspects of Walker's artistic approaches or critical discussions of her work. The "Primary Sources" section lists collected works, recordings, and uncollected writings such as interviews, essays, letters, book and movie reviews, short fiction, and poetry. Secondary compilations feature bibliographies and indexes, biographical articles, unpublished dissertations, articles, essays, and reviews of Walker's works.

The section "General Criticism" contains articles which include critical comments covering multiple primary sources or which discuss Walker in conjunction with other contemporary writers. Reviews are grouped under the titles of the works discussed, which are arranged chronologically according to the titles' dates of publication. The list of articles and essays is followed by "Miscellany," which lists general articles detailing highlights of Walker's career or which include her only in a peripheral sense. Publishers' notes and other brief acknowledgements, generally, have been excluded. Also, because of the increasing number, anthologies featuring reprints of Walker's works have been omitted from the listings.

Because of the lag in publication of literary indexes, it was extremely difficult to complete secondary sources for 1984 through 1986. Therefore, we explored electronic databases for these years in instances where the sources suggested that they might be useful to our research. Although on-line searching has not been fully developed for database sources in the humanities, these explorations served to provide some current data and enhance the usefulness of the bibliography. Within the confines of these limitations, every effort has been made to make the compilation as extensive and exhaustive as possible.

Our special thanks to M. Marie Foster for her professional acumen exercised in editing this volume and to Charlotte Hunt for serving as a liaison to Walker. We are indebted, also, to Elizabeth Milliken and Donna Graves for their proficiency and enthusiasm in processing our many interlibrary loan requests in an expeditious manner. Moreover, the updating of material was facilitated by Ella Woodbury, who took a personal interest in our project. And, finally, this volume would not be possible were it not for Pamela W. Graham, Nancy W. Bradley, and Novella F. Brown, who typed the preliminary draft, and Cynthia W. McBride, who worked diligently and efficiently to prepare the final draft and insure accurate, neat copy.

THE FLORIDA AGRICULTURAL AND MECHANICAL UNIVERSITY — LOUIS H. PRATT

THE STATE LIBRARY OF FLORIDA — DARNELL D. PRATT

AUGUST 1987

Introduction

Langston Hughes was impressed with Alice Walker's unique creative talent when he commented in 1966 that he had never "read a story like 'To Hell With Dying' before." Subsequently, Walker has written eleven books and received numerous honors and accolades. But it was not until 1983 that she won the American Book Award, shed her mantle of obscurity at 39, and became, in her own words, "a name brand." This was the year that _The Color Purple_ held a place on the New York Times' Best-sellers List for over twenty-five weeks; it was the year Walker became the first Black woman to win the prestigious Pulitzer Prize for fiction.

The long road to fame began for Alice Walker at the tender age of eight when she was blinded accidentally in one eye. As Walker recalls the experience, the scar tissue left her with the psychological trauma of feeling unattractive, isolated, and lonely. However, the turning point came when she decided to focus her attention outward, to observe people, to sharpen her sensitivity, her sensibilities, to the life around her. Walker recorded the tales of the grownups in the neighborhood and she made use of those stories in her later writings.

This same sense of urgency and isolation also provided the psychological context for her first book of poetry, _Once_. In _Interviews With Black Writers_, Walker recalls in detail her su-icidal state and her desperate need to create which, ultimately, began to prevail. Alice Walker wrote of diverse experiences which grew out of her sojourn in Africa, her ideas about life and love and death, the hostilities and frustrations suffered in the small coastal community of Liberty County, Georgia, and the "joy I felt when I could leave each vicious encounter or confrontation whole," in contrast to the fragmented souls, her tormentors, who clearly had entered the ranks of those who were lost.

Walker's survival "whole" and her eventual creative triumph can be traced to the influence of her mother, who provided the time and space for Alice to think, to dream, to create. According to Mary Helen Washington's analysis in "I Sign My Mother's Name," Minnie Lue Walker understood the need for nurturing the creative spirit, and she insisted on her daughter's "absolute right to her own thoughts and feelings." Intuitively, Mrs. Walker allowed Alice to choose her literary pursuits over the household chores whenever the occasion seemed to demand it, and she invested her meager earnings in a sewing machine, a suitcase, and a typewriter, each of which could be manipulated to serve her daughter's creative needs. These gifts were concrete manifestations of "permission" for Alice to assume "the power to create through language, to define [herself] by the written word, to become [witness] to the special sensibility of black women."

Walker recalls her college years at Spellman as inhibiting

and restrictive, and although she found a greater independence at Sarah Lawrence, she decided after graduation that she had been "miseducated." In "The Unglamorous But Worthwhile Duties of the Black Revolutionary Artist," Walker discusses her exposure to Keats, Byron, and Frost, and she laments the "blind spots in her education" such as the total absence of Langston Hughes, Arna Bontemps, Gwendolyn Brooks, and Margaret Walker. She remembers the South of Flannery O'Connor and William Faulkner, and she deplores the exclusion W. E. B. DuBois' _Black Reconstruction_ and Jean Toomer's _Cane_ from her reading lists. She decides that these writers studied in college would be of minimal use in helping her to assume her "duty as a black poet." At this point Walker rejects the premise that art and politics must remain separate entities, and she reaches the conclusion that her art must be pressed into the service of a political end: the liberation of Black people. Subsequently, intellectual curiosity led her to recognize and appreciate her cultural forebears, but her most startling discovery was Zora Neale Hurston, whom Walker now acknowledges as her literary progenitor.

What fascinated Walker was that Hurston had a complete, undiminished sense of self. Having been reared in the all-Black town of Eatonville, Florida, Hurston had benefitted from this sense of self-sufficiency engendered by her background. Consequently, Hurston's community role models had arrogantly conferred their authorial permission on her imaginative pursuits. In "Zora Neale Hurston: A Cautionary Tale and A Partisan View," Walker refers to her as a "cultural revolutionary... who gave us racial health; a sense of Black people as complete, complex, undiminished human beings." Walker found in Hurston an unequivocal pride in the totality of her Blackness and all that it signified. Thus, she fiercely admired Hurston's independence and her straightforward manner which prevailed as she "followed her own road, believed in her own goals, pursued her own dreams, and refused to separate herself from 'common' people."

Having read Hurston's Mules and Men, Walker began to formulate her own artistic philosophy, according to her recollections in "The Unglamorous But Worthwhile Duties of the Black Revolutionary Artist." Walker argues that the Black writer must maintain contact with the people, revere cultural forebears, repeal hatred and protect the heritage from its destructive powers, and present man as "neither good nor beautiful," but as a real human being. Simultaneously, she counsels that "the artist. . .is the voice of the people, but she is also The People." Here Walker also cautions the writer against labels, and she recommends the validity of the works themselves, instead of the categorization or descriptions superimposed upon them.

Though Alice Walker is wary of artistic labels, she is

quick to acknowledge her heritage as a Southern Black woman. For the most part, it is the South that provides the settings for her novels, poetry, and short stories which often describe violence, injustice, and brutality. Walker contends that these themes reflect the innate depravity of America, which she attempts to analyze from a moral perspective. Consequently, in "A Child of the South," Walker contends that the South is symbolic of ". . .a moral center that is absolutely bedrock to the land."

Alice Walker, as writer/poet/seer, looks beyond the physical landscape and probes into the violence to calculate the human damage which prevents the "spiritual survival" of her people. She admires the courage, stamina, and persistence of Southern Blacks, especially their ancestors, and she stands in awe of the mystery of their survival. Thus, she insists on the sacredness of family relationships. Walker admonishes Blacks that the love and emotional support provided by the family are crucial for survival amid the insidious, pervasive racism which still runs rampant in America today. These recognitions suggest the more complex dimension of Alice Walker as seer. Having survived the poverty suffered by her family, Walker acknowledges in "Writing to Survive" that she has a "radical vision of society, and that the way I see things can help people see what needs to be changed."

For Walker, this prophetic role has led her to examine

some of the interrelationships within the family: fathers and daughters and husbands and wives. Her favorite theme is the plight of the Black woman who has been restricted, psychologically and physically, from transferring the enormous ingenuity used to create magnificent quilts, grow splendiferous flower gardens, and tell intriguing stories into the full spectrum of human endeavor--the release of her creative energy in untraditional ways. She attacks the social prejudice which Frances Ellen Watkins Harper protested near the turn of the century in her poem, "Double Standard," and she urges women to diversify and offer their talents to the world. Riding the crest of the wave of feminism, Walker rejects this appellation and describes the new awareness as "womanism," a term aptly suited to the Black culture. She remains a staunch advocate of "bonding," the collective effort of women for pooling their considerable talents and sharing their emotional stability to provide sustenance and support for each other in their struggle for freedom.

A brief survey of Walker's characters also reveals evidence of her commitment to change: Grange Copeland reclaims his humanity between his first and third lives, Celie gains an awareness of self and the possibilities for employing her creative talents, and Albert learns to respect his fellow human beings and follow his innate perceptions and inclinations. Too, Meridian changes toward the end of the novel as she passes her responsibilities on to Truman Held. Sometimes, however, the changes wreak havoc, as in the case of Mem, who is reduced by Brownfield as near to his level as he can manage, and then she dies rather than abandon the last shred of dignity left to her. And there is the fiesty Sophia, proud and uncompromising in her demands for human dignity and respect, who is physically abused and maimed by a system which fails to recognize her rights as a human being.

Not only does Walker recommend change in the lives of her characters and her society, but she is also willing to apply that dictum to her own life as well. As she recalls in "Alice Walker Makes the Big Time,"

> Before I thought that I could move people to change by showing them violence and what it could do. But some people don't necessarily learn by seeing the hard, the harsh and the ugly. So I decided I should try to show good people who struggle--and survive.

The result of this decision was the publication of her popular novel, _The Color Purple_, and the filming of the book into a movie of the same name, both of which have received substantial critical attention.

Indeed, the entire range of Walker's work has been subjected to close scrutiny. Many readers identify with her persistence in championing the causes of women as a double minority, and they revel in her courage to describe a reality not unlike their own. Others praise her keen perceptions, her sharply-drawn characters, and her consummate ability to tell a good story. Beyond the praise, however, have been whirlwinds of controversy as Walker's detractors have emerged from both sexes and among all races and persuasions. Some would have her books banned in Boston (and elsewhere), while others view her as a cultural enemy, a traitor to be burned at the literary stake of censorship. These critics have continued to ask why Walker has chosen to create a superabundance of kind, loving women who triumph in spite of the odds, played off against weak, violent men who fail to celebrate their own humanity as well as recognize that humanity in others. They have deplored Walker's negative images of Black males at a time when these portrayals threaten to undermine the Black family which is already struggling to survive. Such are the polarities surrounding Walker's art.

Yet, Alice Walker continues to practice her craft and insist on her right to challenge the status quo and examine the depths of her personal experiences which have shaped her vision of the male in general. And, as she readily admits in "Brothers and Sisters," those experiences have been negative:

> I desperately needed my father and brothers to give me male models I could respect, because white men...whether in films or in person...offered man as dominator, as killer, and always as hypocrite.
>
> My father failed because he copied the hypocrite. And my brothers--except for one

> --never understood they must represent half the world to me, as I must represent the other half to them.

There is an admirable honesty and openness here that critics have often overlooked in their search for positive Black role models which, unquestionably, are prerequisites for self-esteem. On the other hand, however, it seems equally certain that while Walker's men are atypical of Black males in general, these characters are reflective of those male models in her own life. Therefore, these are the images which she presents to her readers.

Impartiality suggests the need for not only extending freedom to the critic who is intent on pursuing a particular point of view, but also to the writer who is committed to examining a unique vision of life. Consequently, it is not reasonable to suggest the dismissal of a talented writer such as Alice Walker on the basis of her perceptions alone. For in spite of her biases (such as afflict us all), she has many messages to convey: preserve cultural heritage and traditions, honor the family, eradicate injustice and violence, preserve and extend human freedoms, allow women to revel in their own diversity, cultivate honesty, accept the inevitability of change, and permit the human spirit to dominate, survive, and prevail.

ALICE MALSENIOR WALKER

An Annotated Bibliography: 1968-1986

Primary Sources

BOOKS

Novels

The Color Purple. New York: Harcourt, Brace, Jovanovitch, 1982.

Meridian. New York: Harcourt, Brace, Jovanovitch, 1976.

The Third Life of Grange Copeland. Harcourt, Brace, Jovanovitch, 1970.

Short Stories and Readers

I Love Myself When I Am Laughing -- And Then Again When I Am Looking Mean and Impressive. Edited by Alice Walker. Old Westbury, New York: Feminist Press, 1979.

In Love and Trouble: Stories of Black Women. New York: Harcourt, Brace, Jovanovitch, 1973.

You Can't Keep A Good Woman Down: Stories. New York: Har-Court, Brace, Jovanovitch, 1981.

Poetry

Five Poems. Detroit: Broadside Press, 1972.

Good Night, Willie Lee, I'll See You in the Morning: Poems. New York: Dial Press, 1979.

Horses Make a Landscape Look More Beautiful. New York: Harcourt, Brace, Jovanovitch, 1984.

Once: Poems. New York: Harcourt, Brace, Jovanovitch, 1968.

Revolutionary Petunias and Other Poems. New York: Harcourt, Brace, Jovanovitch, 1973.

Essays and Biography

In Search of Our Mothers' Gardens: Womanist Prose. San Diego: Harcourt, Brace, Jovanovitch, 1983.

Langston Hughes, American Poet. New York: Crowell, 1974.

OTHER WORKS

Interviews

"Alice Walker." In *Black Women Writers At Work*, Edited by Claudia Tate, pp. 175-187. New York: Continuum Publishing Company, 1983.

"Alice Walker." In *Interviews With Black Writers*, Edited by John O'Brien, pp. 184-211. New York: Liveright, 1973. Rptd. in *Mothers' Garden* as "From An Interview."

"Alice Walker: Her Mother's Gifts." Interview by Mary Helen Washington. *Ms.* 10, No. 12 (June 1982): 38.

"Alice Walker Makes the Big Time with Black Folk Talk." Interview by Pam Abramson. *California Living* (15 August 1982):

16-20.

"American Scholar Forum: Women on Women." Interview of eight women writers by Hiram Hayden. _The American Scholar_ 41, No. 4 (Autumn 1972): 599-622.

"An Interview With Alice Walker." Interview by Jessica Harris. _Essence_ 7, No. 3 (July 1976): 33.

Anon. "The Hum Inside the Skull: A Symposium." _New York Times Book Review_ (13 May 1984): 1 ff.

Anon. "A Survey: Black Writers Views On Literary Lions and Values." _Negro Digest_ 17, No. 3 (January 1968): 10-17.

"Characters in Search of a Book." Interview by Ray Anello. _Newsweek_ 99, No. 25 (21 June 1982): 67.

"A Child of the South, a Writer of the Heart." Interview by Jacqueline Trescott. _Washington Post_, August 8, 1976, pp. G1, G3.

"A Conversation With Alice Walker." Interview by Sharon Wilson. _Kalliope_ (1984): 37-45.

"Eudora Welty: An Interview." _Harvard Advocate_ 106 (Winter 1973): 68-72.

"First Novelists." Edited by Irene Stokvis Land. _Library, Journal_ 95, No. 12 (15 June 1970): 2299.

"Writing to Survive: An Interview with Alice Walker." Interview by Krista Brewer. _Southern Exposure_ 9, No. 2 (Summer 1981): 12-15.

Essays and Letters

"Addendum: Treating the Earth Like Dirt." Wilderness 48 (Summer 1984): 42. (Excerpt from "When A Tree Falls," Ms. January, 1984).

"Alice Walker's Reply" [to Lani M. Nolan's letter on "Anais Nin: 1903-1977"]. Ms. 6, No. 2 (August 1977): 8. (See entry number 414.)

"Alice Walker's Reply" [to Rev. Donald J. O'Leary's letter, "On the Diary of an African Nun"]. Freedomways 9, No. 1 First Quarter 1969): 71-73. (See entry number 415.)

"Am I Blue?" Ms. 15, No. 1 (July 1986): 29-30.

"America Should Have Closed Down on the First Day a Black Woman Observed that the Supermarket Collard Greens Tasted Like Water." Ms. 13, No. 7 (January 1985): 53-54.

"Anais Nin: 1903-1977." Ms. 5, No. 10 (April 1977): 46.

"Beyond the Peacock: The Reconstruction of Flannery O'Connor." Ms. 4, No. 6 (December 1975): 77-79 ff. Rptd. in Mothers' Gardens.

"The Black Woman's Story." New York Times Magazine, Section 6 (12 February 1984): 94. (Walker's reply to David Bradley's article, "Novelist Alice Walker: Telling the Black Woman's Story," which appeared in the January 8 issue.)

"The Black Writer and the Southern Experience." New South 25, No. 4 (Fall 1970): 23-26. Rptd. in Mothers' Gardens.

"But Yet and Still the Cotton Gin Kept on Working." The Black

Scholar 1, Nos. 3-4 (January/February 1970): 17-21. Rptd. in *The Black Scholar* (September/October 1983) and *Mothers' Gardens*.

"Can I Be My Brother's Sister?" (by Straight Pine). *Ms*. 4, No. 4 (October 1975): 64-67ff. Rptd. in *Mothers' Gardens*.

"China." *Ms*. 13, No. 9 (March 1985): 51-52ff.

"The Civil Rights Movement: What Good Was It?" *American Scholar* 36, No. 4 (Autumn 1967): 550-554. Rptd. in *Mothers' Gardens*.

"The Color Purple." *The Wall Street Journal* 207, No. 8 (13 January 1986): 27. (See entry number 317.)

"The Color Purple Didn't Come Easy." *San Francisco Chronicle Book Review* (October 10, 1982): 1ff. Rptd. in *Mothers' Gardens* as "Writing *The Color Purple*."

"Embracing the Dark and the Light." *Essence* 13, No. 3 (July 1982): 67 ff. Rptd. in *Mothers' Gardens* as "If the Present Looks Like the Past, What Does the Future Look Like?

"Father: For What You Were." *Essence* 16, No. 1 (May 1985): 93-94ff.

"Finding Celie's Voice." *Ms*. 14, No. 6 (December 1985): 71-72ff.

"Foreword to *Zora Neale Hurston: A Literary Biography*" by Robert Hemenway. Urbana: University of Illinois Press, 1977. Rptd. in *Mothers' Gardens* as "Zora Neale Hurston: A Cautionary Tale and a Partisan View" and in *Freedomways*

(Third Quarter 1978) as "Complex and Contradictory Life."

"The Growing Strength of Coretta Scott King." _Redbook_ 137, No. 5 (September 1971): 96-97ff. Rptd. in _Mothers' Gardens_ as "Coretta King: Revisited."

"In the Closet of the Soul." _Ms_. 15, No. 5 (November 1986): 32-33 ff.

"In Search of Our Mothers' Gardens." _Ms_. 2, No. 11 (May 1974): 64ff. Rptd. in _Mothers' Gardens_ and in _Claims for Poetry_, Edited by Donald Hall. Ann Arbor: University of Michigan Press, 1982.

"In Search of Zora Neale Hurston." _Ms_. 3, No. 9 (March 1975): 74-76ff. Rptd. in _Mothers' Gardens_ as "Looking for Zora" and in _Between Women: Biographers, Novelists, Critics, Teachers and Artists Write About Their Work on Women_. Edited by Carol Ascher, Louise De Salvo, and Sarah Ruddick. Boston: Beacon Press, 1984.

"Jean Toomer." _New York Times Book Review_, Section 7 (17 August 1980): 25.

"A Letter to the Editor of _Ms_.: On the Founding of the National Black Feminist Organization." _Ms_. 3, No. 2 (August 1974): 4. Rptd. in _Mothers' Gardens_.

"Letters Forum: Anti-Semitism." _Ms_. 11, No. 8 (February 1983): 13ff.

"Lulls." _The Black Scholar_ 7, No. 8 (May 1976): 3-12. Rptd. in _Ms_. (January 1977) and _Mothers' Gardens_.

"My Father's Country is the Poor." New York Times (March 21, 1977): 27. Rptd. in The Black Scholar (Summer 1977), Ms. (September 1977) as "Secrets of the New Cuba" and in Mothers' Gardens.

"Nuclear Exorcism: Beyond Cursing the Day We Were Born." Mother Jones Journal 7, No. 8 (September/October 1982): 20-21. Rptd. in Mothers' Gardens as "Only Justice Can Stop a Curse."

"One Child of One's Own: A Meaningful Digression Within the Work(s)." Ms. 8, No. 2 (August 1979): 47-50ff. Rptd. in The Writer on Her Own Work, Edited by Janet Sternburg. New York: W. W. Norton and Company, 1980, and in Mothers' Gardens.

"Other Voices, Other Moods." Ms. 7, No. 8 (February 1979): 50-53ff. Rptd. in Mothers' Gardens as "Looking to the Side, and Back."

"Redemption Day. Mother Jones 11, No 9 (December 1986): 43-45.

"Silver Writes." U. S. Commission on Civil Rights. Perspectives: The Civil Rights Quarterly 14 (1982): 22. Rptd. in Mothers' Gardens.

"Staying at Home in Mississippi: Ten Years After the March on Washington." New York Times Magazine, Section 6, Part 1 (26 August 1973): 9ff. Rptd. in Mothers' Gardens as "Choosing to Stay at Home: Ten Years After the March on Washington."

"The Strangest Dinner Party I Ever Went To." _Ms_. 11, Nos. 1-2 (July/August 1982): 58ff.

"A Talk by Alice Walker '65: Convocation 1972." _Sarah Lawrence Alumni Magazine_, Summer 1972. Rptd. in _Mothers' Gardens_ as "A Talk: Convocation 1972."

"Uncle Remus, No Friend of Mine." _Southern Exposure_ 9, No. 2 (Summer 1981): 29-31.

"The Unglamorous but Worthwhile Duties of the Black Revolutionary Artist, or of the Black Writer Who Simply Works and Writes." _The Black Collegian_ 2, No. 1 (September/October 1971): 5ff. Rptd. in _Mothers' Gardens_.

"View from Rosehill Cemetery: A Tribute to Dr. Martin Luther King, Jr." _South Today_ 4 (1973): 11. Rptd. in _Mothers' Gardens_ as "Choice: or A Tribute to Dr. Martin Luther King, Jr."

"When a Tree Falls." _Ms_. 12, No. 7 (January 1984): 48ff.

"When the Other Dancer is the Self." _Ms_. 11, No. 11 (May 1983): 70ff. Rptd. in _Mothers' Gardens_ as "Beauty: When the Other Dancer is the Self."

"When Women Confront Porn at Home." _Ms_. 8, No. 8 (February 1980): 67-70ff.

Book and Movie Reviews

"The Almost Year." _New York Times Review_, Section 7, (11 April 1971): 22. (Reviews Florence Engel Randall's _The Almost_

Year.) Rptd. in *Mothers' Gardens*.

"Another Life." *The Village Voice* 19, No. 15 (11 April 1974): 26. (Reviews Derek Walcott's *Another Life*.)

"Black Anima." *Parnassus* 2, No. 2 (Spring/Summer 1974): 5-14. (Reviews N. J. Loftis' *Black Anima*.)

"The Black Scholar Book Review." *The Black Scholar* 8, No. 3 (December 1976): 51-52. (Reviews Rosa Guy's *Ruby*.)

"Black Sorority Bankrolls Action Film." *Ms*. 4, No. 12 (July 1976): 45. (Reviews "Countdown at Kusini," produced by Delta Sigma Theta, directed by Ossie Davis.) Rptd. in *Mothers' Gardens*.

"Books: Who's Reading What: 45 Books that Changed 16 Minds." *Ms*. 6, No. 1 (July 1977): 33. (Reviews *One Hundred Years of Solitude*, *Their Eyes Were Watching God*, and *The Bush Rebels*.)

"Breaking Chains and Encouraging Life." *Ms*. 8, No. 10 (April 1980): 35ff. (Reviews *Conditions: Five, The Black Women's Issue*, edited by Lorraine Bethel and Barbara Smith.) Rptd. in *Mothers' Gardens*.

"Can't Hate Anybody and See God's Face." *New York Times Book Review*, Section 7 (29 April 1973): 8. (Reviews June Jordan's *Fannie Lou Hamer*.)

"A Daring Subject Boldly Shared." *Ms*. 3, No. 10 (April 1975): 120ff. (Reviews Ann Allen Shockley's *Loving Her*.)

"The Divided Life of Jean Toomer." *New York Times Book Review*,

Section 7 (13 July 1980): 11ff. (Reviews _The Wayward and The Seeking: A Collection of Writings By Jean Toomer_, edited with an introduction by Darwin T. Turner.) Rptd. in _Mothers' Gardens_.

"The Friends." _New York Times Book Review_, Section 7 (4 November 1973): 23. (Reviews Rosa Guy's _The Friends_.)

"Gifts of Power: The Writings of Rebecca Jackson." _The Black Scholar_ 12, No. 5 (September/October 1981): 64-67. (Reviews _Gifts of Power: The Writings of Rebecca Jackson (1795-1871), Black Visionary, Shaker Eldress_, edited with an introduction by Jean McMahon Humez.) Rptd. in _Mothers' Gardens_.

"Good Morning Revolution." _The Black Scholar_ 7, No. 10 (July/August 1976): 53. (Reviews Langston Hughes' _Good Morning Revolution: Uncollected Writings of Social Protest_.) Rptd. in _Mothers' Gardens_.

"Jane Didn't Stay in a Corner." _New York Times Book Review_, Section 7 (23 May 1971) 6ff. (Reviews Ernest Gaines' _The Autobiography of Miss Jane Pittman_.)

"Like the Eye of a Horse." _Ms_. 11, No. 12 (June 1974): 41-42. (Reviews Ai's _Cruelty_.)

"Nuclear Madness: What Can You Do?" _The Black Scholar_ 13, Nos. 2-3 (Spring 1982): 81. (Reviews Helen Caldicott's _Nuclear Madness: What Can You Do?_) Rptd. in _Mothers' Gardens_.

"A Walk Through 20th Century Black America." Ms. 8, No. 6 (December 1979): 46ff.

"A Writer Because of, Not in Spite of Her Children." Ms. 4, No. 7 (January 1976): 40ff. (Reviews Buchi Emecheta's Second Class Citizen.) Rptd. in Mothers' Gardens.

Short Fiction

"The Abortion." Mother Jones 5, No. 8 (August 1980): 30ff. Rptd. in Good Woman.

"Advancing Luna -- and Ida B. Wells." Ms. 5, No. 11 (July 1977): 75-76ff. Rptd. in Good Woman.

"Cuddling." Essence 16, No. 3 (July 1985): 74-76ff.

"The Diary of an African Nun." Freedomways 8, No. 3 (Summer 1968): 226-229. Rptd. in Love and Trouble.

"The First Day (A Fable After Brown)." Freedomways 14, No. 4 (Fourth Quarter 1974): 314-316.

"How Did I Get Away With Killing One of the Biggest Lawyers in the State?" Ms. 9, No. 5 (November 1980): 72-73ff. Rptd. in Good Woman as "How Did I Get Away With Killing One of the Biggest Lawyers in the State? It Was Easy."

"Kindred Spirits." Esquire 104, No. 2 (August 1985): 106-107ff.

"Laurel." Ms. 7, No. 5 (November 1978): 64-66ff. Rptd. in Good Woman.

"A Letter of the Times, or Should This Sado-Masochism Be Saved?"

Good Woman. Rptd. in Ms. as "A Letter of the Times" (October 1981): 63-64.

"The Lover." Good Woman. Rptd. in Essence (April 1981): 87ff.

"Meridian." Essence 7, No. 3 (July 1976): 35-40ff.

"1955, Or, You Can't Keep a Good Woman Down." Ms. 9, No. 9 (March 1981): 54ff. Rptd. in Good Woman as "Nineteen Fifty-five."

"Olive Oil." Ms. 14, No. 2 (August 1985): 35-36ff.

"The Revenge of Hannah Kemhuff." Ms. 2, No. 1 (July 1973): 70-72ff. Rptd. in Love and Trouble.

"Sojourner." Ms. 4, No. 11 (May 1976): 67-71ff.

"Something You Done Wrong." Mother Jones Journal 7, No. 5 (June 1982): 32-35ff.

"A Sudden Trip Home." Essence 2, No. 5 (September 1971): 58ff. Rptd. in Good Woman as "A Sudden Trip Home in the Spring."

"The Third Life of Grange Copeland." Redbook 137, No. 1 (May 1971): 173-195.

"To Hell With Dying." Love and Trouble. Rptd. (condensed) in Readers Digest (October 1983): 110-114 and in Readers Digest [Canadian] (May 1985): 116-120.

Poetry

"The Abduction of Saints." Freedomways 15, No. 4 (Fourth Quarter 1975): 266-267. Rptd. in Willie Lee.

"Burial." Harper's Magazine 244, No. 1462 (March 1972): 73.

Rptd. in *Revolutionary Petunias*.

"The Diamonds on Liz's Bosom." *Vanity Fair* 47 (September 1984): 1984): 110. Rptd. in *Horses*.

"Did This Happen to Your Mother? Did Your Sister Throw Up a Lot?" *Ms*. 6, No. 8 (February 1978): 41. Rptd. in *Willie Lee*.

"Each One, Pull One." *Freedomways* 20, No. 2 (Second Quarter 1980) 87-89. Rptd. in *Horses*.

"Every Morning." *Horses*. Rptd. in *Ladies Home Journal* 102, No. 5 (May 1985): 103.

"Facing the Way." *Freedomways* 15, No. 4 (Fourth Quarter 1975): 265-266. Rptd. in *Willie Lee*.

"Family Of." *Freedomways* 21, No. 1 (First Quarter 1981): 46-47. Rptd. in *Horses*.

"For My Sister Molly." *Harper's Magazine* 244, No. 1462 (March 1972): 72. Rptd. in *Revolutionary Petunias*.

"Forgive Me If My Praises." *The Black Scholar* 10, Nos. 3-4 (November/December 1978): 46. Rptd. in *Willie Lee*.

"Forgiveness." *Freedomways* 15, No. 4 (Fourth Quarter 1975): 267. Rptd. in *Willie Lee*.

"Gift." *Essence* 3, No. 3 (July 1972): 60. Rptd. in *Revolutionary Petunias*.

"Gray." *Callaloo* 2, No. 5 (February 1979): 63. Rptd. in *Horses*.

"How Poems Are Made: A Discredited View." *Vanity Fair* 47

(September 1984): 110. Rptd. in _Horses_.

"I Must Whistle Like a Woman Undaunted." _Essence_ 15, No. 6 (October 1984): 90. (Excerpts from _Horses_.)

"I'm Really Very Fond." _Ms_. 7, No. 10 (April 1979): 21. Rptd. in _Horses_.

"If Those People Like You." _Ms_. 7, No. 10 (April 1979): 21. Rptd. in _Horses_.

"Janie Crawford." _The Black Collegian_ 9, No. 5 (May/June 1979): 93. Rptd. in _Willie Lee_.

"Judith Jamison." _Ms._ 1, No. 11 (May 1973): 66-67.

"Malcolm." _The Black Collegian_ 9, No. 5 (May/June 1979): 93. Rptd. in _Willie Lee_.

"Listen." _Family Circle_ 97, No. 16 (13 November 1984): 68. Rptd. in _Horses_.

"Mississippi Winter II." _Vanity Fair_ 47, (September 1984): 110. Rptd. in _Horses_.

"Mississippi Winter III." _Vanity Fair_ 47. (September 1984): 110. Rptd. in _Horses_.

"My Daughter is Coming." _Callaloo_ 2, No. 5 (February 1979): 33. Rptd. in _Horses_.

"New Face." _Revolutionary Petunias_. Rptd. in _Essence_ 14, No. 7 (November 1983): 122.

"Overnights." _Callaloo_ 2, No. 5 (February 1979): 109. Rptd. in _Horses_.

"Poem at Thirty-Nine." _Ms_. 11, No. 12 (June 1983): 101. Rptd.

in *Horses*.

"Rock Eagle." *Freedomways* 11, No. 4 (Fourth Quarter 1971): 367. Rptd. in *Revolutionary Petunias* as "Eagle Rock."

"South." *Freedomways* 11, No. 4 (Fourth Quarter 1971): 368.

"Talking to My Grandmother Who Died Poor Some Years Ago (While Listening to Richard Nixon Declare 'I Am Not A Crook.'") *The Black Scholar* 6, No. 9 (June 1975): 62. Rptd. in *Willie Lee* as "Talking to My Grandmother Who Died Poor (While Listening to Richard Nixon Declare 'I Am Not A Crook.'") and in *The Black Scholar* (November/December 1981).

"Thief." *Essence* 3, No. 3 (July 1972): 60. Rptd. in *Revolutionary Petunias*.

"When Golda Meir Was In Africa." *The Black Scholar* 10, Nos. 6-7 (March/April 1979): 8. Rptd. in *Ms*. (April 1979) and in *Horses*.

"Women." *Essence* 11, No. 1 (May 1980): 102. Rptd. in *Revolutionary Petunias*.

"When We Held Our Marriage." *Nimrod* 21, Nos. 2-22 (1977): 296.

"Your Soul Shines." *Willie Lee*. Rptd. in *Nimrod* 21, Nos. 2-22 (1977): 296.

Cassette Tapes

Alice Walker Interview. (1 7/8 ips, mono, 47 min.). Columbia Missouri: American Audio Prose Library, 1981.

Alice Walker Reading "Nineteen Fifty-Five" and Interview. (2 cassettes, range: 36½ - 46:20 min.). Columbia, Missouri: American Prose Library, 1981.

Alice Walker: The Color Purple. (1 7/8 ips, 2-track, mono, 60 min.). Los Angeles: Pacifica Tape Library, 1982.

Alice Walker, Writer. (mono). Swarthmore College, April 7, 1981.

A Cautionary Tale. (2 track, mono). Urbana, Illinois: National Council of Teachers of English, 1977.

A Celebration of Black Women in Literature. (1 7/8 ips, 2-track, mono, 29 min.). Washington: National Republic Radio, 1980.

Literature of the Black Experience. (1 7/8 ips). Washington: National Public Radio, 1981.

Writing About Women's Lives. (1 cassette, 29 min., 33 sec.) Washington: Feminist Radio Network, 1970.

Secondary Sources

Bibliographies and Indexes

1. Bell, Roseann P., Betty J. Parker, and Beverly Guy-Sheftall, editors. *Sturdy Black Bridges: Visions of Black Women in Literature.* Garden City, New York: Anchor Press/Doubleday, 1979, pp. 379-405.
   Presents an extensive general bibliography on selected Black women writers, as well as primary and selected secondary sources for twenty-four individual Black women writers from Phillis Wheatley to Alice Walker.

2. Callenbach, Jessamine S., Compiler. *Index to Black American Literary Anthologies.* Boston: G. K. Hall and Company, 1979, p. 106.
   Provides index to anthologies which include Walker's poetry and short stories.

3. Davis, Lenwood G., Compiler. *The Black Woman in American Society: A Selected Annotated Bibliography.* Boston: G. K. Hall and Company, 1975, p. 52.
   Discusses the theme of *In Love and Trouble: Stories of Black Women* in annotated bibliographical entry.

4. Fairbanks, Carol and Eugene A. Engeldinger, Compilers. *Black American Fiction: A Bibliography.* Metuchen,

New Jersey: The Scarecrow Press, Inc., 1978, pp. 278-280.
Lists Walker's novels and short fiction, with selective entries for criticism and reviews of her writings.

5. Fifer, Elizabeth. "A Bibliography of Writings by Alice Walker." _Contemporary Women Writers_. Edited by Catherine Rainwater. Lexington, Kentucky: University Press of Kentucky, 1985, pp. 165-171.
Contains primary sources which include books, short stories, poems, articles, and reviews.

6. French, William P., Michel Fabre, and Amritjit Singh, Editors. _Afro-American Poetry and Drama, 1760-1975_. Detroit: Gale Research Company, 1979, pp. 25, 239.
Gives abbreviated listing of primary and secondary sources.

7. Kirschner, Susan. "Alice Walker's Nonfictional Prose: A Checklist, 1966-1984." _Black American Literature Forum_ 18, No. 4 (Winter 1984): 162-163.
Provides comprehensive listings of Walker's essays and lectures, reviews, letters, and miscellaneous writings.

8. Margolies, Edward and David Bakish, Editors. _Afro-American_

Fiction, 1853-1976: A Guide to Information Sources. Detroit: Gale Research Company, 1979, pp. 96, 101. Focuses on CLA Journal (December, 1975) and O'Brien's Interviews with Black Writers which contain information on Walker's art.

9. Reardon, Joan and Kristine A. Thorsen, Compilers. Poetry by American Women, 1900-1975: A Bibliography. Metuchen, New Jersey: Scarecrow Press, 1975, p. 507. Provides complete listings for Once and Revolutionary Petunias.

10. Rush, Theressa G., Carol F. Myers, and Esther S. Arata, Editors. Black American Writers: Past and Present. Metuchen, New Jersey: Scarecrow Press, 1975, pp. 727-729.
Lists Walker's collected and uncollected writings, with a brief selection of criticism and reviews.

11. Ward, Jerry W. Jr. "Selected Bibliography for the Study of Southern Black Literature in the Twentieth Century." Southern Quarterly 23, No. 2 (Winter 1985): 94-115.
Recommends bibliographies, periodicals, books, and articles on literary background, history, and criticism. Lists primary sources and selected critical references for seventy-eight individual Southern

writers.

12. White, Barbara A., Compiler, American Women Writers: An Annotated Bibliography of Criticism. New York: Garland Publishing Company, 1977, p. 11.
Gives a brief annotation for Walker's article, "In Search of Our Mothers' Gardens."

Biographical Articles

13. Bannon, Barbara. Publishers' Weekly 198, No. 9 (31 August 1970): 195-197.
Focuses on Walkers' early years, family, college, marriage, and breakthrough into publishing.

14. Christian, Barbara. "Alice Walker." Dictionary of Literary Biography, Volume 33. Edited by Thadious M. Davis and Trudier Harris. Detroit: Gale Research Company, 1984, pp. 258-271.
Presents a discussion of the major influences on Walker's writings: her life at Spelman and Sarah Lawrence Colleges, her female ancestors, her familiarity with other Black writers and writers from other countries. Explores the themes of all her works through The Color Purple. Includes brief secondary bibliography.

15. Commire, Ann, Editor. Something About the Author, Volume 31. Detroit: Gale Research Company, 1983, pp. 177-179.
Presents brief details of Walker's life and career. Concentrates on recollections made by Walker concerning her early education, family, life, and artistic philosophy.

16. Directory of American Poets, 1975 Edition. New York: Poets and Writers, Inc., 1974, p. 62.
Gives a thumbnail listing of Walker's current address and writings in poetry and fiction.

17. Evans, Mari, Editor. "Alice Walker." Black Women Writers (1950-1980): A Critical Evaluation. Garden City, New Jersey: Anchor Press/Doubleday, 1984, pp. 494-495.
Provides brief listing of personal data, awards and honors, and primary and secondary sources.

18. Evory, Ann, Editor. Contemporary Authors, First Revision, Volume 37-40. Detroit: Gale Research Company, 1979 pp. 582-583.
Focuses on brief biographical data, primary and selected secondary bibliography. Summarizes Walker's view that racism in American society threatens to destroy the sacred family relationships of Black

people.

19. McDowell, Margaret B. "Alice Malsenior Walker." _Contemporary Novelists_, Fourth Edition. Edited by D. L. Kirkpatrick. New York: St. Martin's Press, 1986, pp. 844-846.
Summarizes biographical and professional details of Walker's life, presents a listing of her books, and offers a brief, general discussion of her novels.

20. Mitgang, Herbert. "Alice Walker Recalls the Civil Rights Battle." _New York Times Biographical Service_ 14, No. 4 (April 1983): 500.
Recalls Walker's years as a civil rights activist and college student. Recounts briefly the artistic process of her American Book Award-winning novel, _The Color Purple_.

21. Moritz, Charles, Editor. _Current Biography Yearbook_. New York: H. W. Wilson Company, 1984, pp. 430-433.
Presents a succinct biographical sketch, along with interspersed comments and quotations from reviewers which typify the critical reception received by Walker's writings.

22. Page, James A., Compiler. _Selected Black American Authors: An Illustrated Bio-Bibliography_. Boston: G.

K. Hall and Company, 1977, p. 277.
Includes biographical, career, and professional information, as well as an abbreviated bibliography of primary and secondary sources.

23. Page, James A. and Jae Min Roh. _Selected American, African, and Caribbean Authors: A Bio-Bibliography_. Littleton Colorado: Libraries Unlimited, 1985, pp. 282-283.
Includes general biographical details and a primary bibliography.

24. Ploski, Harry and James Williams, Editors. _The Negro Almanac_, 4th edition. New York: John Wiley and Sons, 1983, p. 1000.
Presents a brief biographical sketch which includes a listing of Walker's writings.

25. Shockley, Ann Allen and Sue P. Chandler, Editors. _Living Black American Authors_. New York: R. R. Bowker, 1973, p. 163.
Presents a brief listing of biographical information and professional experiences.

26. Steinem, Gloria. "Do You Know This Woman? She Knows You: A Profile of Alice Walker." _Ms_. 10, No. 12 (June 1982): 35ff. Rptd. as "Alice Walker: Do You

Know This Woman? She Knows You" in her *Outrageous Acts and Everyday Rebellions*. New York: Holt, Rinehart, and Winston, 1986.
Discusses Walker's attitudes toward Black women's struggles, her artistic philosophy, and her life in general.

27. Walters, Marian. "Alice Walker." *Contemporary Authors: New Revision Series*, Vol. 9. Edited by Ann Evory and Linda Metzger. Detroit. Gale Research Company, 1983, pp. 514-517.
Details significant aspects of Walker's career as writer of poems, novels, and short stories. Includes primary and selected secondary sources, as well as informative digest of current critical opinion on Walker's work, which depicts "familiar people who struggle for survival of self in hostile environments."

28. *Who's Who Among Black Americans*, 3rd edition. Northbrook, Illinois: Who's Who Among Black Americans, Inc., 1981, p. 814.
Offers thumbnail biographical listing of Walker's achievements.

29. *Who's Who In America*, 38th edition (1974-75), Vol. 2. Chicago: Marquis Who's Who, Inc., 1974, p. 3191.

Presents a thumbnail biographical sketch and a brief listing of primary bibliographical sources.

30. *Who's Who In America*, 39th edition (1976-77), Vol. 2. Chicago: Marquis Who's Who, Inc., 1976, p. 3259. Contributes extremely brief biographical, bibliographical, and professional data.

31. *Who's Who In America*, 40th edition (1978-79), Vol. 2. Chicago: Marquis Who's Who, Inc., 1978, p. 3357. Summarizes briefly Walker's biographical data and contributes biographical and professional listings.

32. *Who's Who of American Women*, 8th edition (1974-75). Chicago: Marquis Who's Who, Inc., 1973, p. 1000. Presents a thumbnail sketch of Walker's life and writings.

Unpublished Dissertations

33. Dawson, Emma J. Waters. "Images of the Afro-American Female Character in Jean Toomer's *Cane*, Zora Neale Hurston's *Their Eyes Were Watching God* and Alice Walker's *The Color Purple*." Dissertation, University of South Florida, 1987. USF, 1987

Traces the depiction of the Afro-American woman in fiction through three novels over a period of fifty-nine years. Concludes that Toomer's women are invisible, passive stereotypes whose individuality is never acknowledged by their men, while Hurston's heroine finally achieves self-actualization through her relationships with the men in her life. However, Walker's female protagonist becomes the first Black Black woman who begins to define herself in terms of her own creativity and versatility.

34. Gaston, Karen Carmean. "The Theme of Female Self-Discovery in the Novels of Judith Rossner, Gail Godwin, Alice Walker, and Toni Morrison." Dissertation, Auburn University, 1980.
Explores the theme of self-discovery through the use of female characters engaged in a quest for meaning in their lives. These women become victims of guilt, fear, and social myths which impede their progress along the path of growth and self-knowledge.

35. Kearns, Katherine Sue. "Some Versions of Violence in Three Contemporary American Novels: John Irving's *The World According to Garp*, Tim O'Brien's *Going After Cacciato*, and Alice Walker's *The Color Purple*." Dissertation, University of North Carolina at Chapel Hill, 1982.
Discusses specific types of violence as phenomena in

contemporary American life: rape, murder, assassination, racism, sexism, incest, and war. Argues that this pervasive corruption threatens characters on every level in these novels and reveals the fundamentally violent nature of our society.

36. Malone, Gloria Snodgrass. "The Nature and Causes of Suffering in the Fiction of Paule Marshall, Kristin Hunter, Toni Morrison, and Alice Walker." Dissertation, Kent State University, 1979. KSU, 1979
Analyzes the nature and extent of human pain and suffering by revealing characters who experience exploitation, demoralization, poverty, racism, sexual abuse, neo-colonial oppression, and domestic discord. Contends that the central theme of suffering becomes an essential, inevitable facet of existence which unifies exploited peoples of the world.

37. White, Vernessa Cecelia. "A Comparative Study of Alienation, Identity, and the Development of Self in Afro-American and East German Fiction." Dissertation, State University of New York at Binghamton, 1981.
Approaches the novels of Toni Morrison and Alice Walker, contrasted with those of Hermann Kant and Guenter De Bruyn, as works produced in countries with antipodal social and political views. In spite of

these dissimilarities, White concludes that these novels reflect the existence of racial prejudice in East Germany as well as America, and that the oppressive system of racial discrimination in America has its roots in the European system of privileges extended on the basis of class distinctions.

General Criticism

38. Anon. "Alice Walker: Going Her Own Way." *Vanity Fair* 46 (April 1983): 91.
Views Alice Walker as ahead of her time, as was Zora Neale Hurston, Nella Larsen, and Jean Toomer. Considers her novels and poems as efforts to "retrieve discarded bits of black culture as they fall from fashion."

39. Anon. "Black Women Novelists: New Generation Raises Provocative Issues." *Ebony* 40, No. 1 (November 1984): 59ff.
Praises the work of Alice Walker, Toni Morrison, Ntozake Shange, Gayl Jones, Toni Cade Bambara, Paule Marshall, and Gloria Naylor as significant contributions to the literature of Black people.

40. Barksdale, Richard K. "Castration Symbolism in Recent American Fiction." *College Language Association*

Journal 29, No. 4 (June 1986): 400-413.
Analyzes Black male victimization in Gayle Jones' *Eva's Man* and *Corregidora*, Toni Morrison's *Sula*, and Alice Walker's *The Color Purple*. Criticizes the negative role models presented by these writers, but acknowledges that these women are limited by their experiences and observations.

41. Bell, Roseann P. "Judgement: Addison Gayle." *Sturdy Black Bridges: Visions of Black Women in Literature*. Edited by Roseann P. Bell, Betty J. Parker, and Beverly Guy-Sheftall. Garden City, New York: Anchor Press/Doubleday, 1979, pp. 210-216.
Reports remarks made by Addison Gayle concerning Gayl Jones, Toni Morrison, and Alice Walker. Argues that these "modern writers" have used their novels as vehicles for a vitriolic assault on Black men without realizing that Black women have been victimized by their attacks.

42. Bradley, David. "Telling the Black Woman's Story." *New York Times Magazine* (8 January 1984): 25-37.
Balances penetrating quotations from several interviews with critical comments about Walker's writings. Presents an insightful view of Walker's early life and her artistic philosophy.

43. Bryfonski, Dedria, Editor. _Contemporary Literary Criticism_, Volume 9. Detroit: Gale Research Company, 1978, pp. 557-558.

Presents brief sampling of criticism on _Meridian_, _The Third Life of Grange Copeland_, and _Revolutionary Petunias_.

44. Callahan, John F. "Reconsideration: The Higher Ground of Alice Walker." _The New Republic_ 171, No. 11 (14 September 1974): 21-22.

Reviews _Once_, _The Life of Grange Copeland_, _Revolutionary Petunias_, and _In Love and Trouble_. Recognizes the influence of Toomer and Hurston and argues that Walker's major theme is that the downtrodden must become responsible for their interactions with each other.

45. Christian, Barbara. "Trajectories of Self-Definition: Placing Contemporary Afro-American Women's Fiction." _Conjuring: Black Women, Fiction, and Literary Tradition_. Edited by Majorie Pryse and Hortense Spillers. Bloomington: Indiana University Press, 1985, pp. 233-248.

Describes and analyzes the various stages experienced by Afro-American women novelists in order to reach the themes of the 1980's which show a concern for the exploration and development of self. Lauds the traditions of earlier novelists whose work has been indispensable to the current trend of viewing the Black woman as a central, rather than a marginal figure.

46. Cliff, Michelle. "'I Found God in Myself and I Loved Her/ I Loved Her Fiercely': More Thoughts on the Work of Black Women Artists." _Journal of Feminist Studies in Religion_ 2 (1986): 7-39.
Focuses on "fierceness" as an African image associated with Black women and explores the concept of femininity as a characteristic of the Deity. Traces the visual art of Afro-Americans, particularly women, to the creativity of their African forebears.

47. Cornish, Sam. "Alice Walker: Her Own Woman." _Christian Science Monitor_ (3 February 1984): B1, ff.
Reviews _In Search of Our Mothers' Gardens_, _The Color Purple_, _You Can't Keep A Good Woman Down_, _Meridian_, _In Love and Trouble_, _Revolutionary Petunias_, _The Third Life of Grange Copeland_, and _Once_. Traces the influence of Zora Neale Hurston on Walker and concludes that Walker's writings are charming, sincere, and absorbing.

48. Davis, Thadious M. "Alice Walker." _Dictionary of Liter-_

ary Biography: American Novelists Since World War II, Second Series, Volume 6. Edited by James M. Kibler, Jr. Detroit: Gale Research Company, 1980, pp. 350-358.
Focuses on Walker's artistic philosophy and presents a critical analysis of *The Third Life of Grange Copeland* and *Meridian*. Argues that Walker's unique contribution lies in her "illumination of art in society, of the artist in ordinary people...."

49. Donovan, Josephine. "Toward a Women's Poetics." *Tulsa Studies in Women's Literature* 3 (1984): 98-110.
Isolates six intra-cultural phenomena which have functioned to define and inform the world view of women, as opposed to that of men. Calls for a gynocentric approach to the criticism of work by women writers which will "enable women today and in the future to see, to express, to name their own truths."

50. Fisher, Berenice. "Guilt and Shame in the Women's Movement: The Radical Ideal of Action and Its Meaning for Feminist Intellectuals." *Feminist Studies* 10 (1984): 185-212.
Refers briefly to *Meridian* in advancing the argument that rather than deny our conflicting voices, we should examine and analyze them as vehicles for re-

leasing our creative and critical voices and for providing more genuine insight into the validity of our ideals.

51. Guntor, Sharon R., Editor. <u>Contemporary Literary Criticism</u>, Volume 19. Detroit: Gale Research Company, 1981, pp. 450-456.
Discusses "The Diary of an African Nun," "A Sudden Trip Home in the Spring," <u>The Third Life of Grange Copeland</u>, and <u>Meridian</u> in brief, perceptive excerpts of criticism of Walker's exploration of intra-family relationships."

52. Hernton, Calvin. "The Sexual Mountain and Black Women Writers." <u>Black American Literature Forum</u> 18, No. 4 (Winter 1984): 139-145. Rptd. in <u>The Black Scholar</u> (July/August, 1985).
Argues that traditional male dominance of the Black literary world has resulted in the subordination of the experiences of the Black female. Contends that during the decade of the 1970's the work of Black female writers paved the way for a Black feminist perspective and a supporting aesthetic "in which the form, languages, syntax, sequence, and metaphoric rendering of experience are markedly different and expansive..." from the literature of their male coun-

terparts.

53. Homans, Margaret. "'Her Very Own Howl': The Ambiguities of Representation in Recent Women's Fiction." _Signs_ 9, No. 2 (Winter 1983): 186-205.
Contends that the experiences of women can be expressed adequately through language, on the one hand, and that, paradoxically, there is also a need for creating new alternative forms of expression. Includes references to the novels of Marilyn French, Monique Wittig, Toni Morrison, Margaret Atwood, Alice Walker, and Margaret Drabble.

54. Howard, Lillie P. "Alice Walker." _American Women Writers_, Volume 4. Edited by Lina Mainiero. New York: Frederick Ungar Publishing Company, 1982, pp. 313-315.
Presents biographical sketch and brief comments on _Revolutionary Petunias_, _The Third Life of Grange Copeland_, _In Love and Trouble_, _Langston Hughes_, and _Meridian_, which are praised as honest and engaging. Also includes brief, selective primary and secondary bibliographies.

55. Marcus, Laura. "Feminism into Fiction: The Women's Press." _Times Literary Supplement_ (27 September 1985): 1070.
Reviews several "feminist novels" designed to counteract the female stereotypes popularized by male

writers and create a women's history and myth.

56. Miller, Jane. "Women's Men." In her Women Writing About Men. London: Virago Press Limited, 1986, pp. 227-263.
Analyzes male-female interrelationships from the viewpoint of women whose novels attest to their experiences as victims of multiple oppression. Focuses on selected works of Toni Morrison, Paule Marshall, Alice Walker, Tillie Olsen, and Maxine Hong Kingston.

57. Ogunyemi, Chikwenye Okonjo. "Womanism: The Dynamics of the Black Female Novel in English." Signs II, No. 1 (Autumn 1985): 63-80.
Uses selected novels to argue the thesis that African and Afro-American women are distinctly united in their writings by their sensitivity to considerations beyond sexism, such as race, culture, economics, and politics.

58. O'Meally, Robert G. New York Times (30 March 1986): Section 7, p. 18.
Praises Pryse and Spillers' Conjuring: Black Women, Fiction, and Literary Tradition for popularizing recent fiction by Toni Morrison, Alice Walker, and other Black women writers whose work has generally been undervalued or ignored.

59. Pemberton, Gayle R. "Black Women Writers." The New York Times (27 July 1986): Section 7, p. 21.
Refers to Mel Watkins' article (New York Times, June 15, 1986) in lamenting the frequent substitution of social for literary concerns when Black critics review works written by other Blacks. Argues that among Black writers, women have brought variety, while the men have propagated the naturalism popularized by Richard Wright.

60. Popkin, Michael, Editor. Modern Black Writers. New York: Frederick Ungar Publishing Company, 1978, pp. 443-446.
Presents a collage of criticism which offers insightful comments on Once, The Third Life of Grange Copeland, Revolutionary Petunias, In Love and Trouble, and Meridian.

61. Pryse, Majorie. "Zora Neale Hurston, Alice Walker and the 'Ancient Power' of Black Women" (Introduction) Conjuring: Black Women, Fiction, and Literary Tradition. Edited by Marjorie Pryse and Hortense Spillers. Bloomington: Indiana University Press, 1985, pp. 1-24.
Traces the question of literary authority in Black writing to Charles Chesnutt, who uses Aunt Peggy as

a source of power. Contends that Zora Neale Hurston used Aunt Peggy's conjuring in Mules and Men as a springboard for establishing literary authority for black writers. Praises Walker for continuing this tradition in her writings -- most notably, The Color Purple -- and for capitalizing on "folk magic as art and fiction as a form of conjuring."

62. Rampersad, Arnold. "Adventures of Huckleberry Finn and Afro-American Literature." Mark Twain Journal 22, No. 2 (Fall 1984): 47-52.
Explores The Adventures of Huckleberry Finn as a precursor of Afro-American fiction and argues that Twain anticipates later Black fiction through his presentation of the moral dilemma faced by Huck. Contends that Twain's depiction of folk culture, dialect, humor, and alienation in American society presaged the work of significant Black writers such as Zora Neale Hurston, Ralph Ellison, Alice Walker, Richard Wright, Ann Petry, James Baldwin, and Toni Morrison.

63. Riley, Carolyn and Phillis C. Mendelson, Editors. Contemporary Literary Criticism, Volume 5. Detroit: Gale Research Company, 1976, pp. 476-477.
Summarizes selected criticism on The Third Life of Grange Copeland and In Love and Trouble.

64. ________. *Contemporary Literary Criticism*, Volume 6. Detroit: Gale Research Company, 1976, pp. 553-554.
Presents a brief summary of representative criticism on *The Third Life of Grange Copeland*, *Once*, and *In Love and Trouble*.

65. Rumens, Carol. "Heirs to the Dream." *Times Literary Supplement* 133, No. 4 (18 June 1982): 676.
Praises Walker for her narrative technique and effective symbolism in *Meridian* and *You Can't Keep A Good Woman Down* which suggest the writings of Toni Morrison. Argues that the best of Walker's work transcends sexual and racial politics to bring to life "the varied scents and colours of human experience."

66. Sanford, Barbara D. and Karima Amin. *Black Literature for High School Students*. Urbana: National Council of Teachers of English, 1978, pp. 88-90.
Presents brief summaries of *Revolutionary Petunias and Other Poems*, *In Love and Trouble: Stories of Black Women*, and *Meridian*.

67. Schultz, Elizabeth. "Out of the Woods and into the World: A Study of Interracial Friendships Between Women in American Novels." *Conjuring: Black Women, Fiction, and Literary Tradition*. Edited by Marjorie Pryse

and Hortense Spillers. Bloomington: Indiana University Press, 1985, pp. 67-85.

Contends that interracial friendships in fiction by women and by white men are established as protests to the dominant racism in American society. Praises Walker and Toni Morrison as pioneers in establishing the thesis that the denunciation of racial stereotypes provides the foundation for friendships between women of different races.

68. Sorel, Nancy. "A New Look at 'Noble Suffering'." The New York Times Book Review, Section 7 (26 January 1986): 1 ff.

Discusses 18th, 19th, and 20th century writings on childbirth by men and women writers. Views Meridian and In Search of Our Mothers' Gardens as statements on childbearing as a "noble suffering."

69. Spillers, Hortense J. "Cross Currents, Discontinuities: Black Women's Fiction." (Afterword) Conjuring: Black Women, Fiction, and Literary Tradition. Edited by Marjorie Pryse and Hortense Spillers. Bloomington: Indiana University Press, 1985, pp. 249-261.

Maintains that women's fiction acknowledges the power of the community as it speaks directly to the people. Predicts that future writings will continue to dramatize and reflect the struggles of a people for survival and triumph.

70. Taylor, Clyde. "Black Writing as Immanent Humanism." _The Southern Review_ 21, No. 3 (July 1985): 790-800.
Uses Richard Wright's 1937 essay, "Blueprint for Negro Writing," as a criterion for examining Wright's prophetic view of Black writing as a dynamic force for human liberation. Notes that although Wright did not anticipate the "womanist perspective" as a powerful, creative force, literature by Black women has promoted a new configuration of the humanism which he advocated. Emphasizes the need for a new blueprint which can predict trends in Black writing for the next half century.

71. Walker, Cam. _Southern Exposure_ 5, No. 1 (Spring 1977): 102-103.
Argues that _Meridian_ lacks the unity and coherence of _The Third Life of Grange Copeland_, but concludes that the character Meridian is seen by the reader as "another memorable black woman."

72. Washington, Mary Helen. "I Sign My Mother's Name: Alice Walker, Dorothy West, Paule Marshall." _Mothering the Mind: Twelve Studies of Writers and Their Silent Partners_. Edited by Ruth Perry and Martine Watson

Brownley. New York: Holmes and Meier, 1984, pp. 142-163.

Contends that the common bond shared by Dorothy West, Paule Marshall, and Alice Walker is the role played by each writer's mother in stimulating her creative and artistic talents.

73. __________. "Introduction." In her edited anthology, _Black-Eyed Susans: Classic Stories By and About Black Women_. Garden City, New York: Anchor Press/Doubleday 1975, pp. xi-xxii.

Concentrates on dispelling stereotypes about Black women, with attention to the works of Toni Morrison, Nella Larsen, Zora Neale Hurston, Gwendolyn Brooks, Dorothy West, Ann Petry, Paule Marshall, and Margaret Walker. Emphasizes Alice Walker's short story, "A Sudden Trip Home in the Spring," as a "reconciliation between black men and black women, ... between the past and present."

74. Williams, Delores S. "Women's Oppression and Lifeline Politics in Black Women's Religious Narratives." _Journal of Feminist Studies in Religion_ I, No. 1 (1985): 59-71.

Affirms the concept that the "religious narratives" of Zora Neale Hurston, Margaret Walker, and Alice

Walker reveal assaults on Black women's reproductive/ nuturing ability, physical beauty, and productive relationships. Discusses strategies developed by Afro-American women for resisting these attacks.

Book and Movie Reviews

Once. New York: Harcourt, Brace, Jovanovitch, 1968.

75. Anon. *The Booklist* 65, No. 9 (1 January 1969): 474.
Analyzes the poems as impressionistic reflections of Walker's experiences in the United States, Africa, and the Soviet Union.

76. Anon. *Publishers' Weekly* 194, No. 7 (12 August 1968): 49.
Views this collection of poems as refined and poignant. Argues that Walker's talent lies in her ability to feel love and to communicate that love through her art.

77. Benedict, Estelle. *Library Journal* 93, No. 16 (15 September 1968): 3145.
Assesses Walker's work as sensitive extrapolations of her experiences which "succeed in evoking in the reader all the concurrent images that go with the thoughts she has expressed."

78. Mueller, Lisel. "Versions of Reality." _Poetry_ 117, No. 5 (February 1971): 322-330.
Considers Walker's work and the poetry of seven other artists. Views Walker's writings as honest, direct, sharp, and sensitive creations which reveal the historical implications of the ever-present consciousness of color.

79. Rodgers, Carolyn M. _Negro Digest_ 17, Nos. 11,12 (September/October 1968): 52 ff.
Praises Walker for her precise language and the power generated by her informal tone and straightforward approach. Suggests that these poems, like Black people, are "explosions of love, hate, fear, joy, sorrow, _Life_."

80. Walsh, Chad. "A Present Rooted in the Past." _Book World_ 2, No. 44 (3 November 1968): 20.
Sees a tension in the poems created by sensitive expressions of tenderness, juxtaposed to the overwhelming brutality of the world.

The Third Life of Grange Copeland. New York: Harcourt, Brace, Jovanovitch, 1970.

81. Anon. _Kirkus Reviews_ 38, No. 13 (1 July 1970): 711.
Reports this novel as an extraordinarily painful

narrative which focuses on three generations of Black Georgia sharecroppers who attempt to survive in a white-oriented society.

82. Anon. Publishers' Weekly 197, No. 21 (25 May 1970): 55-56.
Reviews The Third Life of Grange Copeland as a true picture of Southern Black family life.

83. Coles, Robert. "Books to Try Men's Souls." The New Yorker 47, No. 2 (27 February 1971): 104-106.
Contends that Walker's depiction of the life of a Black sharecropper's family who has suffered from the oppression of white society makes her a storyteller for all times.

84. Cornish, Sam. Essence 1 (April 1971): 2.
Regards the novel as a portrayal of courageous Black women who cope with the white and Black worlds without losing consciousness of their Blackness. Criticizes Walker for inclusion of the "bootstrap theory" but contends that the book is "one of the most important Black novels we have."

85. Cunningham, Valentine. "Over the Rainbow." The Observer (3 November 1985): 25.
Assesses the tension in the novel as a product of the dismal choices offered the characters: white, estab-

lishment-style bondage on one hand, as opposed to wine, women, and withdrawal on the other. Considers the women characters "savior figures" who insure posterity of the Black race.

86. Glastonbury, Marion. "Of the Fathers." New Statesman 110, No. 2485 (4 October 1985): 28-29.
Reviews The Third Life of Grange Copeland along with three other novels and concludes that The Third Life embodies two of Walker's literary commitments: celebration of our ancestors and our roots and recognition of the struggle/success motif of the slave narrative.

87. Hairston, Loyle. "Work of Rare Beauty and Power." Freedomways 11, No. 2 (Second Quarter 1971): 170-177.
Alludes briefly to Gorky's Mother in comparison with Walker's novel. Contends that the theme of The Third Life is that men who lose their sense of dignity and self-worth also lose their respect for humanity in general.

88. Halio, Jay L. "First and Last Things." The Southern Review 9, No. 1 (January 1973): 455-465.
Reviews the novel along with three others. Argues that Grange has learned to accept a moral responsibility for his actions and that he has tried unsuc-

cessfully to teach this lesson to Brownfield. Sees Ruth as a symbol of the hope for posterity who will avoid the mistakes and the bitterness of the two previous generations.

89. Hendin, Josephine. Saturday Review 53, No. 34 (22 August 1970): 55-56. Describes The Third Life of Grange Copeland as a novel whose themes are "the depletion of love and the erosion of the sources of affection." The men in this novel are shown as self-hating villians who have no capacity for love. On the other hand, the women are heroines who have the ability to love deeply, even though they are savagely mistreated by the men.

90. Kramer, Victor A. Library Journal 95, No. 13 (July 1970): 2522.
Points out how dreams are crushed for two generations of a Black Sharecropping family in Georgia whose only hope is symbolized by the third generation granddaughter. Identifies this plot as a valid picture of Black life in Georgia in the 1920's.

91. McDonnell, Jane. "Contemporary Black Themes: Social, Historical, Hopeful." Cross Currents 21, No. 4 (Fall 1971): 453-475.
Argues that the novel avoids advocating Black Power

on the one hand, while it explains the necessity for this concept in the lives of those who feel inferior or beaten down on the other.

92. Marcus, Greil. "January White Sale." Rolling Stone (26 January 1978): 55.
Discusses the destruction of children by their fathers in three generations of the Copeland Family. Touches on the idea that the Black man's oppression of his wife and children is more horrible than any oppression that white society has caused Blacks, even in slavery.

93. Plumpp, Falvia D. "The Third Life of Grange Copeland." Black Books Bulletin 1, No. 1 (Fall 1971): 26-27.
Describes the novel as a tribute to an individual who has a commitment to improving the lives of future generations.

94. Schorer, Mark. "The Revolving Bookstand...Novels and Nothingness." American Scholar 40, No. 1 (Winter 1970-71): 168-174.
Compares Alice Walker's novel with Dan Wakefield's Going All The Way and Joan Didion's Play It As It Lays. These three novels deal with "essential emptiness of experiences" on three different levels of rural Southern Blacks.

95. Shapiro, Paula Meinetz. "Pygmalion Reversed." The New Leader 54, No. 1 (25 January 1971): 19-20.

Admires Walker's use of the narrative style which allows the characters to speak for themselves. Asserts that she points out the inequities of Southern practices during the period 1920-1960, but allows the reader to make his own assessment of the "...humanity we share rather than the horrors of our dehumanizing experiences."

96. Theroux, Paul. "A Glimpse of Freedom." Book World 4, No. 37 (13 September 1970): 2.

Declares that this is a fictionalized picture of the Black family which bears very little resemblance to reality.

97. Wandor, Michelene, "Family Sagas." Books and Bookmen (October 1985): 42.

Reviews Ntozake Shange's Betsey Brown and Alice Walker's The Third Life of Grange Copeland. Views Walker's novel as a "family saga" of Black men who defy the odds in their struggle for responsibility and independence.

In Love and Trouble: _Stories of Black Women_. New York: Harcourt, Brace, Jovanovitch, 1973.

98\. Anon. _The Booklist_ 70, No. 9 (1 January 1974): 473-474.
Compares the stories with _Revolutionary Petunias and Other Poems_ and argues that each work concerns "ego-bruising experiences." Captures the essence of the Black woman's hardships.

99\. Anon. _The Booklist_ 70, No. 10 (15 January 1974): 538.
Recommends the book for mature teenagers because of its "superior stylistic quality, characterizations, and evocativeness."

100\. Anon. _Choice_ 10, No. 11 (January 1974): 1723.
Praises Walker for her consummate skill in detailing the Black woman's failures and successes in poignant, graphic terms which mirror the reality of a broad range of human experience.

101\. Anon. _English Journal_ 64, No. 9 (December 1975): 80.
Lauds Walker for her perceptiveness in analyzing her characters. Views the women in the stories in their gallant struggles for the achievement of identity and recognition of their personal worth.

102\. Anon. _Kirkus Reviews_ 41, No. 13 (1 July 1973): 712-713.
Views some of the stories as artistic failures but

allows that Walker has a degree of success in "working out possibilities" in the story lines.

103. Anon. The New Republic 171, No. 25 (21 December 1974): 24.
Echoes John Callahan's comments. (See Item Number 44).

104. Anon. Publishers' Weekly 204, No. 1 (2 July 1973): 78:
Declares that the stories present clear evidence of Walker's ability to describe those motivations which bring joy and sorrow in the lives of Black women.

105. Bouise, Oscar A. Bestsellers 33, No. 14 (15 October 1973): 335.
Lauds Walker for her ability to write of the Black woman's experiences in universal terms. Attests to her ability as a "master of styles" who forces the reader into an intimate understanding of her characters.

106. Bryant, Jerry H. "The Outskirts of a New City." The Nation, 217, No. 16 (12 November 1973): 501 ff.
Compares the style and approach of Alice Walker and Ed Bullins (The Reluctant Rapist.) Praises both writers for their determination to forge their own paths and probe into hitherto unexamined aspects of

Black existence.

107. Collier, Betty J. Journal of Social and Behavioral Sciences 21, No. 1 (Winter 1975): 136-142.
Lauds Walker for her role in blazing new trails in Afro-American literature. Focuses on Walker's women who are..."sometimes warm, other times cold, but always human...."

108. Conyus. "Looking Over My Shoulder at the 70's (24 of the Best in the Field)." The Black Scholar 12, No. 2 (March-April 1981): 83.
Describes Walker's volume briefly as "a wonderful collection of stories about Black women."

109. Fowler, Carolyn. "Solid at the Core." Freedomways 14, No. 1 (First Quarter 1974): 59-62.
Praises Walker for her comprehensive exploration of the Black woman's plight in America and for her perceptive portrayals of those human values that we hold in high esteem.

110. Giovanni, Nikki. "So Black and Blue." Book World (18 November 1973): 1.
Maintains that the book has wide appeal because readers can identify with the sincere, genuine, straightforward way in which the problems of Black women are

examined.

111. Goodwin, June. _The Christian Science Monitor_ 64, No. 250 (19 September 1973): 11.
Praises Walker's stories which aptly and skillfully reflect her experiences in the sharecropper's South.

112. Grumbach, Doris. "Fine Print-Twelve Re-views: 1974." _The New Republic_ 171, No. 25 (21 December 1974): 23-24.
Echoes John Callahan's statement that Walker's superior craftmanship is used to create haunting stories which "evoke magnificently diverse lives." (See item number 44.)

113. Ingoldby, Grace. "Fall Out." _New Statesman_ 108, No. 2791 (14 September 1984): 32.
Lauds Walker for the creation of characters who have the capacity for intense feeling, and views these stories as suitable tributes to her African heritage.

114. Kane Patricia. "The Prodigal Daughter in Alice Walker's 'Everyday Use'." _Notes on Contemporary Literature_ 15 (March 1985): 7.
Compares the protagonist in "Everyday Use" with the Biblical prodigal son. Notes, however, that Walker reverses the values of the parents and ends her story

after the mother arrives at a greater appreciation of Maggie, the daughter who has remained by her side.

115. Maginnis, Ruth. *Library Journal* 98, No. 20 (15 November 1973): 3476.
Considers the volume a noteworthy achievement but cautions that readers may be offended by man's inhumanity to his loved ones.

116. Mellors, John. "Fraught Stories." *The Listener* 113, No. 2891 (10 January 1985): 24.
Analyzes eight short story anthologies and concludes that Walker's stories illuminate the plight of women who are "driven by their men into madness and a futile revenge."

117. Minudrl, Regina V. *Library Journal* 98, No. 22 (15 December 1973): 3692.
Views the book as an outstanding collection of stories which describes many aspects of Black womanhood.

118. Nyabongo, V. S. *Books Abroad* 48, No. 4 (Autumn 1974): 787.
Praises the stories for their themes which reflect strong feelings about relations among human beings. Praises Walker for skill and precision in depicting

her male characters.

119. Peden, William. "The Black Explosion." Studies In Short Fiction 12, No. 3 (Summer 1975): 231-241.
Discusses In Love and Trouble in conjunction with selected works of Langston Hughes, Richard Wright, Chester Himes, James Baldwin, Ann Petry, and Cyrus Colter. Views the collection as "the work of a major writer, thoroughly in command of the situation at all times."

120. Pfeffer, Susan Beth. Library Journal 98, No. 14 (August 1973): 2338-2339.
Alludes to an unevenness in quality among the stories which illuminate the social changes experienced by Black women.

121. Smith, Barbara. "The Souls of Black Women." Ms. 2 (February 1974)): 42ff.
Praises Walker for her ability to "explore with honesty the texture and terrors of Black women's lives."

122. Washington, Mary Helen. "Black Women Image Makers." Black World 23, No. 10 (August 1974): 10-18.
Discusses the works of Maya Angelou, Toni Cade Bambara, Gwendolyn Brooks, Paule Marshall, and Alice Walker. Focuses on Walker's short stories, "Rose-

lily" and "Everyday Use," and their respective themes of the promise and disappointment of romantic love and the estrangement from one's roots.

123. ____________. "In Love and Trouble." _Black World_ 23, No. 12. (October 1974): 51-52.
Assesses the stories as a collective, authentic, and successful effort to probe the depths of the Black woman's experiences.

124. Watkins, Mel. _New York Times Book Review_ 123, No. 42, 421, Section 7 (17 March 1974): 40-41.
Views the stories as "perspective miniatures, snapshots that capture their subjects at crucial and revealing moments."

125. Wood, Michael. "Stories of Black and White." _The London Review of Books_ 6 (4 October 1984): 16-17.
Reviews Alice Walker's stories with Angela Carter's _Nights at the Circus_ and Joan Didion's _Democracy_. Acknowledges Walker's ability to write compelling and colorful prose and evoke scenes of Southern life, but laments the "melodramatic dashes of violence" which are evident in the stories.

126. Wright, Mercedes A. "Black Woman's Lament." _The Crisis_ 81, No. 1 (January 1974): 31.

Argues that the stories describe the inner conflicts of Black women in a racist, sexist society. Alleges that this volume established the importance of the women's liberation movement for Black women.

Revolutionary Petunias and Other Poems. New York: Harcourt, Brace, Jovanovitch, 1973.

127. Anon. _Book World_ 8, No. 3 (21 January 1973): 15.
Argues that the poems analyze ethnic roots and explore the tension between love and revolution.

128. Anon. _The Booklist_ 69, No. 19 (1 June 1973): 928.
Praises these autobiographical poems for their graphic descriptions of Walker's roots and for her sensitivity to the need for compassion, trust, and love in human affairs.

129. Anon. _Bulletin for the Center of Children's Books_ 27, No. 6 (February 1974): 103.
Emphasizes the poems which graphically and candidly depict the pain and pleasure of Walker's childhood experiences and praises the writing as "clean... and incisive..."

130. Anon. _Choice_ 10, No. 7 (September 1973): 986.
Describes the poems as piquant and engaging, coming

from "a fresh, new, unafraid voice that should be listened to."

131. Anon. Kirkus Reviews 40, No. 23 (December 1972): 1402.
Analyzes Walker's ability to reveal the complexity of her experience in simple statements of "unelaborated integrity."

132. Anon. Publishers' Weekly 202, No. 25 (18 December 1972): 39.
Applauds Walker for her ability to assess her experiences and convert them into simple, direct, powerful statements.

133. Davis, Gwendolyn. New South 28 (Winter 1973): 62-63.
Commends Walker for her ability to translate the specifics of her childhood experiences into the collective emotional experiences of Black people.

134. Dollard, Peter. Library Journal 98, No. 1 (1 January 1973): 73.
Views the poems as reflections of Walker's childhood remembrances of rural Georgia, adult reactions to Black militancy, and emotional expressions of love.

135. Kenworthy, Duncan. "Contemporary Poetry: Six Touchstones." The American Scholar 42, No. 3 (Summer 1973): 514 ff.

Praises Walker for her strong, sincere, realistic poetry which evolves into an affirmation of hope.

136. Roberts, Mary. Communication Education 27, No. 3 (September 1978): 263.
Considers Walker's poems to be expressions of problems of intercommunication among people of different ages, races, and sexes.

137. Turner, Darwin. "A Spectrum of Blackness." Parnassus 4, No. 2 (Spring/Summer 1976): 202-218.
Presents a comparison/contrast of Walker's poetry with that of Ishmael Reed. Concludes that Walker's poetry reaches a ground of commonality in the "affirmation of blackness and creation of a people."

138. Walsh, Chad. Book World 8, No. 13 (1 April 1973): 13.
Contends that the poems based on Walker's childhood in the South are the most successful ones in the collection.

139. Ward, Jerry W. College Language Association Journal 17, No. 1 (September 1973): 127-129.
Considers Walker's celebration of her black Southern roots to be a means of coping with the frustrations of our contemporary society.

140. Washington, Mary Helen. "Revolutionary Petunias and Other

Poems." *Black World* 22, No. 11 (September 1973): 55 ff.

Analyzes the poems in this collection as a successful effort to explore and interpret the southern Black experience from a woman's vantage point.

Langston Hughes, American Poet. New York: Crowell, 1974.

141. Anon. *Black Books Bulletin* 4, No. 1 (Spring 1976): 56.
Provides interesting summary and recommends the book as an important source for the accomplishments of black people.

142. Anon. *Bulletin of the Center for Children's Books* 28, No. 4 (December 1974): 71.
Describes the biography as a sympathetic depiction of Hughes' early years, a significant book for a reader in the primary grades.

143. Anon. *Elementary Education* 52 (January 1975): 147.
Argues that the discussion of prejudice, racial pride, and family problems is too complex for eight and nine year olds. Recommends the book for ten to thirteen year-old slow readers.

144. Anon. *Kirkus Reviews* 42, No. 6 (15 March 1974): 307
Lauds Walker for her sensitive selection of appropriate

details which result in a precise portrayal of the young poet.

145. Anon. Social Education 39, No. 3 (March 1975): 173.
Lists the biography in an annotated bibliography of the most notable trade books in the field of social studies for 1973 and 1974. Considers the book an incisive analysis for intermediate readers.

146. Anon. Wilson Library Bulletin 48, No. 10 (June 1974): 789.
Mentions the biography briefly as part of a constructive series for children, ages 6-9.

147. Dreyfuss, Joel. "Beyond Booker T." Book World (19 May 1974): 4
Makes extremely brief mention of the book, written by a "master of words."

148. Jenkins, Betty L. Library Journal 99, No. 18 (15 October 1974): 2743.
Praises the book as one which emphasizes Hughes' youth and his relationships with his family.

149. Whitelaw, Nancy. "Where Have the Good Children's Biographies Gone?" Christian Science Monitor 75, No. 120 (13 May 1983): B7.
Discusses the biography as an effective means of

conveying Hughes' sincere and profound racial pride to the reader in grades 2-4.

<u>Meridian</u>, New York: Harcourt, Brace, Jovanovitch, 1976.

150. Adams, Phoebe-Lou. <u>Atlantic Monthly</u> 237, No. 6 (June 1976): 106.
Analyzes Meridian's self-abnegation and describes the work as "angry and moving."

151. Anon. "The Black Scholar Book Previews: Spring 1976." (See Black Books Round-up insert.) <u>The Black Scholar</u> 7, No. 7 (April 1976): [3].
Lauds Walker for her "clear, almost incandescent prose that sings and sears [and] her ability to see the essence of life in all things and take joy in it."

152. Anon. <u>The Booklist</u> 72, No. 18 (15 May 1976): 1320.
Describes the protagonist, Meridian Hill, and her ambivalent feelings about her heritage.

153. Anon. <u>Choice</u> 13, No. 7 (September 1976): 829-830.
Argues that Walker uses her charcters to summarize the civil rights movement in a story where action is "circular, not linear."

154. Anon. <u>Kirkus Reviews</u> 44 (15 March 1976): 348.

Considers the novel to be a "replay [of The Third Life of Grange Copeland] without a firm core." Emphasizes Meridian's commitment to equality for Blacks but finds the other characters peripheral to the story.

155. Anon. New York Times Book Review , Section 7 (29 May 1977): 23.
Finds Meridian's story "facinating for its revelations, admirable for its deft telling."

156. Anon. Progressive 40, No. 10 (October 1976): 60.
Considers the novel as a sensitive portrayal of one woman's struggle to inspire her people to cherish and maintain their dignity and improve their lives.

157. Anon. The Virginia Quarterly Review 52, No. 4 (Autumn 1976): 13.
Objects to Walker's tendency to overstate her evidence and to allow some of the stories to sink into melodrama.

158. Bannon, Barbara A. Publishers' Weekly 209, No. 13 (29 March 1976): 47.
Finds the strength of the novel in Walker's ability to narrate the story through her characters instead of the ideas presented.

159. Burnside, Gordon. _Commonweal_ 104, No. 9 (29 April 1977): 281-285.
Relates Camus' ideology to the civil rights movement of the 60's and argues that _Meridian_ is not a novel but a historical document.

160. Clifford, Gay. "In the Black Light of Noon." _The Times Literary Supplement_ 936, No. 3 (19 August 1977): 1014.
Regards the stature of Meridian as "heroic" because it evolves from "a collective tutelary spirit" rather than an individual consciousness.

161. Cooke, Michael G. "Recent Novels: Women Bearing Violence." _The Yale Review_ 66, No. 1 (Autumn 1976): 146 - 155.
Recalls Ernest Gaines' _The Autobiography of Miss Jane Pittman_ and concludes that _Meridian_ is a melange of experiences which are informed by "a vision of the just person."

162. Jefferson, Margo. "Across the Barricades." _Newsweek_ 87, No. 22 (31 May 1976): 71-72.
Praises the epic quality and the historical prespective in _Meridian_. Notes Walker's eye for hypocrisy, "... eccentricities and subtleties of character...."

163. Larson, Charles R. "Legacy of the Movement: A Woman Who Cares." The National Observer 15 (17 July 1976): 17.

Emphasizes Walker's theme that the civil rights movement of the 1960's spawned a stronger generation who have made a humanistic commitment to all of mankind.

164. Lowe, Cynthia. Black Books Bulletin 4, No. 4 (Winter 1976): 60-61.

Summarizes the traumatic story of Meridian's life and concludes that the novel is both realistic and powerful.

165. Marcus, Greil. "Limits." The New Yorker 52, No. 16 (7 June 1976): 133-136.

Compares Meridian with Camus' The Rebel and views Meridian Hill as a typical rebel, according to Camus, who conceives of justice within the context of something larger than herself.

166. Marr, Virginia W. Library Journal 101, No. 9 (1 May 1976): 1145.

Admires the novel because it destroys racial barriers by revealing the common, universal concerns of humanity.

167. Martin, Ruth. _Bestsellers_ 36, No. 6 (September 1976): 187.

Criticizes Walker for the confusing opening chapters and the awkard use of flashbacks. Finds the story satisfying in terms of reader identification with Meridian, who struggles through poverty and ignorance to discover her identity.

168. Mellors, John. "Caradock's Caves." _The Listener_ 97, No. 2500 (17 March 1977): 350.

Focuses on Meridian's determination to avoid violence in her civil rights struggles and her efforts to discover the best way to advance the cause of Black people.

169. Murray, G. E. _Fiction International_ 6/7 (1976): 171-172.

Views Meridian as the continued development of many of the women portrayed in _In Love and Trouble_. Praises Walker for a sharp, poignant narrative and a story which is both damning and beautiful.

170. Piercy, Marge. _New York Times Book Review_, Section 7 (23 May 1976): 5 ff.

Lauds Walker's precise artistic skill in narrating Meridian's story. Criticizes the lack of motivation for the change in Meridian's character which allows her to consider murder as a tool to be used in the Black civil rights struggle.

171. Rogers, Norma. "Struggle for Humanity." Freedomways 16, No. 2 (Second Quarter 1976): 120-122.
Praises Walker for her ability to illuminate the hostility, violence, and bitterness which act as barriers to human intercourse.

172. Sage, Lorna. "From Pregnancy to Rape." The Observer (March 1977): 28.
Praises Walker for her succinct descriptions of Meridian's failures and triumphs, but deplores the novelist's unsuccessful efforts to make her into a heroine.

173. Smith, Cynthia J. "Black Fiction By Black Females." Cross Currents 24, No. 3 (Fall 1976): 340-343.
Reviews Toni Morrison's Sula and Walker's Meridian. Emphasizes Meridian's conclusion that she must continue to dedicate her life to the principles of the civil rights movement. Concludes that these novels "expand the imaginative dimension of fiction about blacks."

Good Night Willie Lee, I'll See You in the Morning: Poems. New York: Dial Press, 1979.

174. Anon. The Booklist 76, No. 15 (1 April 1980): 1103.
Calls attention to Walker's intense alienation as a Black woman and argues that the structure of these poems reflects a greater degree of reality than her earlier works.

175. Anon. Encore America and Worldwide News 8 (2 April 1979): 50.
Praises Walker for her unflinching, fearless, and honest attempts to analyze and explore herself and the life around her.

176. Anon. Publishers' Weekly 216, No. 5 (30 July 1979): 61.
Argues that Walker speaks for radical changes in the social order and praises the emotional sensitivity of her poetry.

177. Dirda, Michael. "In Praise of Poetry." Book World 9, No. 18 (9 November 1979): 11.
Comments on Walker's clear, crisp style and compares her allegories to Stephen Crane's symbolic story-poems.

178. Ratner, Rochelle. Library Journal 104, No. 13 (July 1979): 1464.

Contrasts the shorter, insightful autobiographical poems with the longer creations which use historical figures as their focal points and provide effective, subtle contrasts in tone.

179. Williamson, Alan. "In a Middle Style." Poetry 135, No. 6 (March 1980): 348-354.
Reviews Good Night Willie Lee, I'll See You in the Morning along with three other volumes as a work which is often banal, although it sometimes manifests Walker's gift for using sensitive images.

180. Wilson, Judith. "Chapters...Recollections." Essence 10, No. 8 (December 1979): 16.
Lauds Walker for her "magical simplicity and spine-chilling directness."

I Love Myself When I Am Laughing ... And Then Again When I Am Looking Mean and Impressive. Introduction by Mary Helen Washington. Old Westbury, New York: Feminist Press, 1979.

181. Anon. Choice 17, No. 4 (June 1980): 538.
Discusses autobiographical selections from Zora Neale Hurston's work and focuses on problems of love instead of problems of race among the people of all-Black Eatonville, Florida.

182. Anon. Ebony 35, No. 3 (January 1980): 24.
Acknowledges the volume as a unique collection of Hurston's writings.

183. Blundell, Janet Boyarin. Library Journal 104, No. 20 (15 November 1979): 2463.
Considers Zora Neale Hurston as the most productive Black woman writer of her era and a major figure in the Harlem Renaissance. Suggests that Hurston's lifestyle, her use of Black dialect, and her unpopular stand against integration produced negative reactions.

184. Kennedy, Randall. "Looking for Zora." New York Times Book Review, Section 7 (30 December 1979): 8 ff.
Finds two important themes in the potpourri of Hurston's writings: the determination of Black women to transcend their circumstances and achieve liberation, and the commitment to assert and confirm the pride and dignity of Black people.

185. Marcus, Jane. Chicago 30 (April 1981): 107-108.
Reviews Hurston's literary achievements and recalls her controversial views on race relations and on the attitudes which she held toward her own blackness.

186. O'Meally, Robert G. "The Cosmic Zora." Book World 9, No. 21 (30 December 1979): 12.
Observes that the excerpts contained in the reader have been "culled from Hurston's books with... love and attention to narrative shape" and attributes Hurston's popularity to writing which is "technically excellent and bursting with life."

187. Rushing, Andrea Benton. "Jumping At The Sun." Callaloo 3, Nos. 1-2 (February-October 1980): 228-230.
Sees this work as a rejuvenation of interest and a reassessment of Zora Neale Hurston's art. Discusses the essays by Alice Walker and Mary Helen Washington as additional gems which make the work worth reading.

188. Wilson, Judith. "Filled With Suprises." Essence 10, No. 10 (February 1980): 17.

Discusses Zora Neale Hurston's impatience with Blacks who cursed their fate instead of working to improve the circumstances of their lives.

You Can't Keep A Good Woman Down: Stories. New York: Harcourt, Brace, Jovanovitch, 1981.

189. Anon. Booklist 77, No. 15 (1 April 1981): 1080-1081.

Acclaims Walker's volume as an excellent collection featuring stories of love or self-expression, viewed from "a distinctly black perspective."

190. Anon. *Kirkus Reviews* 49, No. 5 (1 March 1981): 309.
Recognizes Walker as an extremely talented writer, but takes her to task for preoccupation with sociological, rather than literary concerns. Argues, with some reservation, that love and marriage is Walker's best theme.

191. Anon. *Kliatt Young Adult Paperback Book Guide* 16 (February 1982): 30.
Praises Walker for her "important concerns": the nefarious influence of pornography, the oppression of women, and the use of stereotypes. Contends that Walker's sense of humor comes through in the stories, but she often substitutes social criticism for art.

192. Anon. *Publishers' Weekly* 219, No. 12 (20 March 1981): 56.
Praises Walker's ability to capture simultaneously her Blackness, her femininity, and her humanity.

193. Christian, Barbara. "The Short Story in Process." *Callaloo* 5, Nos. 1-2 (February-May 1982): 195-198.

Contrasts the tone of frustration and struggle in In Love and Trouble with that of "triumphant assertiveness" in You Can't Keep A Good Woman Down. Views Walker's non-traditional forms as "process rather than product."

194. Connor, Elizabeth. Library Journal 106, No. 7 (1 April 1981): 90.
Pays tribute to Walker's "mellifluous and effortless" stories and her "cadent style of writing."

195. Dixon, Melvin. The American Book Review 4 (May 1982): 9-10.
Declares that Walker's artistic gift lies in her abilty to combine ideology and personal experience in her fiction and force the reader to examine hurt, oppression, and sexual alienation.

196. Gilbert, Harriet. New Statesman 104, No. 2680 (30 July 1982): 21.
Assesses the collection as an honest, genuine depiction of the Black woman's struggle to resolve "conflicts of identity and loyalty."

197. Naylor, Carolyn. The Black Scholar 13, No. 2-3 (Spring 1982): 84-85.
Contends that Walker successfully uses her artistic

sensitivity to merge history and fiction as she explores the multi-faceted problems of our society and our world.

198. Piercy, Marge. "The Little Nuances of History." _Book World_ 11, No. 22 (31 May 1981): 11.
Considers the stories to be sophisticated art which reflects Walker's mastery, scope, and control of a wide range of material.

199. Pollitt, Katha. "Stretching the Short Story." _New York Times Book Review_ 130, Section 7 (24 May 1981): 9ff.
Praises Walker for her courage to pursue controversial issues and for her perceptive eye for small details. Criticizes her penchant for portraying Black women who never fail to elicit the reader's sympathy and for leaving loose ends and unanswered questions.

200. Scruggs-Rodgers, Emma. _Sepia_ 31 (May 1982): 18.
Discusses the variety of assertive, independent female characters who refuse to allow society to define the perameters of their lives.

201. Sidenbaum, Art. "Make Shelf Room For Alice Walker." _Los Angeles Times_, Part V (9 April 1981): 16.
Perceives Walker as a writer of skill and versatil-

ity who is engaged simultaneously in the fight against racism and sexism. Considers Walker's stories as evidence of the reemergence of the short story as a popular literary form.

202. Walters, Ray. "Paperback Talk." New York Times Book Review 131, No. 45,280, Section 7 (11 April 1982): 27.
Comments on the fact that some stories are autobiographical, while others reflect the contemporary moral, social, and political issues which confront our world.

203. Wilson, Judith. "Main Events." Essence 12 (July 1981): 17.
Maintains that Walker, atypically, employs controversial issues and offers sharp insights into mundane, familiar themes.

The Color Purple. New York: Harcourt, Brace, Jovanovitch, 1982.

204. Anon. The Booklist 78, No. 16 (15 April 1982): 1042.
Praises Walker for her "jolting and revealing perspective..." and the eloquence of her craft.

205. Anon. Ebony 37, No. 12 (October 1982): 26.
Considers the novel a continuation of the bonding of

Black women. Testifies to Walker's skill as a novelist but criticizes her negative posture toward male-female relationships among Blacks.

206. Anon. Kirkus Reviews 50, No. 8 (15 April 1982): 518. Focuses on the folkloristic aspects of the story which proclaim the indestructibility of love.

207. Anon. "Letters to God Are Postmarked with a Pulitzer." People Weekly 20, No. 26 (26 December 1983): 85, 87. Compares Walker with Maya Angelou and Toni Morrison, discusses biographical details of Walker's life, and argues that her major emphasis is on the brutality and hostility which often exists between Black men and women.

208. Anon. New York Times Book Review (29 May 1983): 29. Views the novel as a vehicle which Walker uses to shed light on many of her earlier themes. (See item number 256.)

209. Anon. The New Yorker 58, No. 29 (6 September 1982): 106. Lauds Walker's creative talent and technique and pronounces the novel "fiction of the highest order."

210. Anon. People Weekly 18 (1 November 1982): 14. Recommends the novel to Blacks and women because of its authentic, poignant use of Black English and its

message of hope in spite of hopelessness.

211. Anon. Publishers' Weekly 221, No. 20 (14 May 1982): 205. Describes Walker's novel as a brilliant achievement which highlights the pain, joy, humor, and bitterness of human existence.

212. Anon. "Visiting Good Friends During the Holidays." Black Enterprise 13, No. 5 (December 1982): 30. Considers the book evidence of Walker's creative energy and talent.

213. Anon. West Coast Review of Books 8 (September 1982): 22. Classifies Walker as a writer with a unique vision and praises the novel as a "remarkable, unforgettable work."

214. Atwood, Margaret. "That Certain Thing Called the Girl-Friend." New York Times Book Review (11 May 1986): 1ff. Explores the superficial portrayal of female relationships in novels from the nineteenth centry to the present. Credits Black women novelists with being among the first to explore the complexities of these friendships and cites Walker's The Color Purple and Toni Morrison's Sula as significant contributions to this growing body of literature.

215. Bardacke, Frances L. "The Book Buff: The Novels of Summer." San Diego Magazine 35 (August 1983): 68-72.
Reviews The Color Purple along with John Le Carre's The Little Drummer Girl and Gabriel Garcia Marquez's Chronicle of a Death Foretold. Argues that Walker has problems with time sequence in the novel as she deals with a mixture of fantasy and realism.

216. Bartelme, Elizabeth. "Victory Over Bitterness." Commonweal 110, No. 3 (11 February 1983): 93-94.
Focuses on the suffering experienced by the women and men who are finally forced to accept the circumstances of their lives.

217. Baumgaertner, Jill. The Cresset 46 (May 1983): 28-29.
Concludes that the strength of the novel lies in the fact that Celie's evolving awareness of self allows her to reach out to the other female characters in a mutual sharing, caring, and understanding of their relationships to God and to each other.

218. Bovoso, Carole. "Main Events: Books." Essence 13, No. 6 (October 1982): 20.
Recognizes the novel as a powerful testimony of the courage of Black women and ranks it as a significant contribution to the literature of our time.

219. Brookner, Anita. "Good Girls and Bad Girls." London Review of Books 5 (2-15 June 1983): 20-21.
Reviews the novel along with eight others. Argues that The Color Purple fails to present a balanced view of the circumstances faced by women in our society.

220. Buckley, Reid. The American Spectator 16 (November 1983): 38-39.
Compares Walker with Eudora Welty and Flannery O'Connor. Criticizes the interjection of lesbianism, questions the legitimacy of the Pulitzer Prize award, but concedes that the novel stands as "a hymn to the power of love."

221. Carr, Anne. Commonweal 111, No. 4 (24 February 1984): 120.
Compares the novel to the short stories of Flannery O'Connor and concludes that both writers transcend theology through the creation of fascinating symbols which facilitate the process of "theological reflections."

222. Derman, Lisa. Boston Review 9 (October 1982): 29.
Criticizes Walker for her diatribes but praises her ability to dramatize the ignominious plight of Black women who survive and overcome the circumstances of

their lives.

223. Farwell, Marilyn R. "A Review of Selected Contemporary Fiction By Women." *Northwest Review* 21, No. 1 (1983): 167-176.
Compares the fiction of Walker and Toni Morrison and affirms Walker's thesis that female relationships extend the hope of salvation to women in particular, as well as to the chauvinistic society in general.

224. Foster, Frances Smith, *New York Times*, Section 7 (9 March 1986): 25.
Contrasts the negative portrayal of the Black family in *The Color Purple* with Thordis Simonsen's *You May Plow Here: The Narrative of Sara Brooks* in an extremely brief reference.

225. Fox-Alston, Jeanne. "Tales of Two Southern Families: Searches for Different Kinds of Freedom." *Chicago Tribune Book World*, Section 7 (1 August 1982): 3.
Considers Walker's idea that men and women must work together to transcend traditional limitations placed upon their relationships and achieve dignity and realize self-worth.

226. Goldstein, William. "The Success of the Paperback *Purple*." *Publishers' Weekly* 228, No. 10. (6 September

1985): 48.

Announces the publication of a mass market edition of _The Color Purple_, to be issued in a first printing of one million copies to coincide with the release of the movie version of the novel during the Christmas season. States that the Washington Square trade paperback edition which has sold one and a quarter million copies in two years will remain in print.

227. Graham, Maryemma. _Freedomways_ 23, No. 4 (Fourth Quarter 1983): 278-280.

Attacks Walker's naive and distorted view that Black men, inherently, are rapacious beings who terrorize and victimize their women and perpetuate female oppression.

228. Gussow, Adam. _Chicago Review_ 34, No. 1 (Summer 1983): 124-126.

Interprets the novel as an exploration of female friendship and quiet, courageous ways in which women lend support and give inspiration to each other in the midst of their suffering. Contends that Walker's language is "incandescent, heated with love and rage, and her vision is clear and hard as cut glass."

229. Guy, David. "A Correspondence of Hearts." _Book World_

12, No. 30 (25 July 1982): 1.
Considers Walker's message in the novel to be the neccessity of abandoning the male-oppressor, female-oppressed struggle in order for each to achieve the highest expression of humanity.

230. Halio, Jay L. "Fiction and Reality." The Southern Review 21, No. 1 (Winter 1985): 204-213.
Examines several novels from the premise that the novel extends the boundaries of reality and extends the boundaries of our lives. Argues that The Color Purple exemplifies this theory by increasing our awareness and making us sensitive to the plight of the realistic characters of Walker's world.

231. Heyward, Carter. "An Unfinished Symphony of Liberation: The Radicalization of Christian Feminism Among White U.S. Women." Journal of Feminist Studies in Religion I, No. 1 (1985): 99-118.
Reviews The Color Purple with four other novels which "reflect...interest in the liberation of women from the perspective of white Christian women." Focuses on Walker's novel as a story of liberation of Celie, Shug, and Albert from the insidious influences of a world devoid of love and compassion.

232. ___________. Religious Studies Review 10, No. 2 (April

1984): 162.

Argues that Walker uses _The Color Purple_ to reduce the theoretical concepts of religious doctrine to viable, utilitarian experiences in the lives of her rural poverty-stricken characters.

233. Hiers, John T. "Creative Theology in Alice Walker's _The Color Purple_. _Notes on Contemporary Literature_ 14, No. 4 (September 1984): 2-3.

Argues that creation theology informs the novel as the characters discover God -- not as a static force, but as a surge of creativity which reveals the significance of selfhood, family, and community.

234. Higgins, Chester A., Sr. "Pulitzer Beginning to Do Something Right." _The Crisis_ 90, No. 6 (July-August 1983): 49.

Concurs in the awarding of the Pulitzer Prize to Walker. Recognizes that while the story accounts for the influence of racism in the lives of the characers, she goes beyond to "....capture with remarkable honesty and candor, the casual and intense relationships of the farm people...."

235. Hitz, Henry. _San Francisco Review of Books_ 7 (Summer 1982): 5.

Interprets the novel as a "translation of the blues

into literature." Praises Walker for her ability to communicate the "nuances of language" with the vigor and vitality that Bessie Smith expressed them in music.

236. Jefferson, Margo. _The Nation_ 235, No. 22 (25 December 1982): 696.
Contends that Walker blends epistolary and Black oral traditions to reveal a panorama of the joys and tribulations of private lives, viewed against current and historical perspectives.

237. Kelly, Ernece B. _College Language Association Journal_ 27, No. 1 (September 1983): 91-96.
Advances the thesis that male domination and oppression of females create victims both of men and women and that love is the only redeeming power which can liberate us and save us from ourselves.

238. Koenig, Rhoda. "Summer Pleasures." _New York_ 17 (July 4-11, 1983): 110 ff.
Lauds the novel as the exhiliarating, stimulating story of Celie's rebirth.

239. Leckey, Dolores. _Commonweal_ 111, No. 4 (24 February 1984): 125.
Focuses on the rich spiritual images which Walker

uses in the novel.

240. Lenhard, Georgann. "Inspired Purple." _Notes on Contemporary Literature_ 14, No. 3 (May 1984): 2-3.
Compares _The Color Purple_ with Evelyn Tooley Hunt's poem, "Taught me Purple." Concludes that even though both protagonists lead uneventful lives and aspire toward rewarding ones, only Walker's Celie learns, towards the end of the novel, that she has been fulfilled.

241. Levin, Amy. "Borrowed Plumage." _Women's Studies_ 12, No. 3 (1986): 297-313.
Analyzes _The Color Purple_ along with several other novels. Contends that Celie and Nettie are able to achieve self-actualization only after they have found direction through Shug and Corrine, whom Levin calls their "adopted" sisters.

242. Modleski, Tanya. _The Minnesota Review_ 23 (Fall 1984): 194-195.
Praises Walker for the clarity of Celie's letters to Nettie but maintains that Nettie's letters are often reduced to a travelogue and, consequently, they fail to convey a sense of warmth and charm associated with Celie's experiences near the end of the novel.

243. Mootry-Ikerlonwu, Maria K. College Language Association Journal 27, No. 3 (March 1984): 345-348.
Praises Walker's authentic use of Black English and her ability to maintain reader interest but criticizes her tendency to create unrealistic characters.

244. Mort, Mary Ellen. "Bleak Birthright, Sustaining Joy." Library Journal 107, No. 12 (1 June 1982): 1115.
Praises Walker for her consummate ability to capture the language of her characters.

245. Prescott, Peter S. "A Long Road to Liberation." Newsweek 99, No. 25 (21 June 1982): 67-68.
Argues that the book is "an American novel of permanent importance" which extols female bonding as a redemptive force for the liberation of women from male domination and oppression.

246. Randall-Tsuruta, Dorothy. The Black Scholar 14, Nos. 3-4 (Summer 1983): 54-55.
Considers characterization as the superior element in the novel and praises Walker's sensitivity to dialect, which converts the language into sheer poetry.

247. Reed, J. D. "Postfeminism: Playing for Keeps." Time 121, No. 2 (10 January 1983): 60-61.

Discusses the work of Walker and seven other "feminist" writers. Focuses briefly on the plot of _The Color Purple_.

248. Rolfe, Rebecca. "Honors for Alice Walker." _Atlanta_ 24, No. 2 (June 1984): 30 ff.
Mentions Walker's selection for the Townsend Prize which honors works of fiction by Georgia-born novelists. Presents synoptic view of _The Color Purple_ and concludes that Walker's art exudes an "organic wholeness" which is richly rewarding for the reader.

249. Rosenfeld, Megan. "Profiles in Purple and Black." _Washington Post_ (15 October 1982): E-1, E-3.
Describes the characters in the novel as people who "break through the nearly overwhelming obstacles of race, sex, class, and poverty to the simple joys of companionship and freedom." Intersperses comments by Walker relating to her artistic commitment to social change, her defense of "Black Folk English," and her depiction of women as lovers.

250. Schaefer, Jay. _San Francisco Review of Books_ 7 (January 1983): 23.
Calls the novel an engaging story of frustration, growth, and change experienced by two poor Black sisters.

251. See, Carolyn. "As All the Oppressed Women Close Ranks, a Whole New Complicated Cosmos is Created." _Los Angeles Times Book Review_ (8 August 1983): 3.
Charges that Walker uses an absurd plot which is offset by her perceived message for women: "close ranks, remember relationships, work for each other, and prevail."

252. Smith, Dinitia, "'Celie, You A Tree'!" _The Nation_ 235, No. 6 (4 September 1982): 181-183.
Maintains that the love and courage manifested in the relationships of Black women serve as a redeeming force for them and their men. Argues that the strength of the book lies in Walker's skillful use of the Black folk idiom.

253. Staples, Brent. "Media-Lashed and Sex-Listed." _New York Times_ (23 March 1986): Section 7, 11.
Reviews Ishmael Reed's _Reckless Eyeballing_ which is considered to be a protest against the negative portrayal of Black men in fiction and drama in general and in _The Color Purple_ in particular.

254. Towers, Robert. "Good Men Are Hard to Find." _New York Review of Books_ 29, No. 13 (12 August 1982): 35-36.
Compares the female characters with those created by Faulkner and Wright and focuses on the unity of

women in the novel as they struggle to resist male oppression and domination. Considers structuring one of Walker's weaknesses, but praises her for the "remarkably expressiveness, color, and poignancy" of the dialect of her characters.

255. Watkins, Mel. "Sexism, Racism and Black Women Writers." _New York Times Book Review_, Section 7 (15 June 1986): 1.
Traces the controversy of Black male images in the fiction of Black women writers to Michele Wallace's _Black Macho and the Myth of the Superwoman_. Cautions Black female writers to avoid negative portrayals of Black males which contribute to generalizations that undermine those works. Challenges Black male writers to explore candidly other aspects of Black life which have not yet been examined in fiction.

256. ___________. "Some Letters Went to God." _New York Times Book Review_ 87 (25 July 1982): 7.
Assesses the novel as a graphic dramatization of alienation and brutality which characterizes the struggle between Black male dominance and Black female independence and assertiveness.

257. Williams, Delores. "What Was Missed: _The Color Purple_." _Christianity and Crisis_ 46, No. 10 (14 July 1986):

230-232.

Bemoans the fact that portrayal of the Black male image has dominated much of the discussion of the novel. Argues that Walker's central message is that women must modify their traditional concepts of God and use their spiritual experiences to facilitate their struggles to overcome female oppression.

In Search of Our Mothers' Gardens: Womanist Prose. San Diego: Harcourt, Brace, Jovanovitch, 1983.

258. Allen, Bruce. Smithsonian 14, No. 10 (January 1984): 133-134.

Praises Walker for her "impressive range" and her assaults on a society which condones racial injustice. Considers her essays on civil rights and women's experiences the most stimulating and lucid in the collection.

259. Anon. Booklist 80, No. 1 (1 September 1983): 22.

Recounts Walker's central themes which reflect her "wealth of experience" and "richness of vision."

260. Anon. "Books About the South." Southern Living 19, No. 1 (January 1984): 84.

Considers these essays to be reflections of Walker's sensitivity to the pain and the joy of her past.

Argues that her wit and charm are clearly reflected throughout the selections.

261. Anon. _Choice_ 21, No. 9 (May 1984): 1311.
Compares Walker's collection with June Jordan's _Civil Wars_ and recommends Walker's essays as a valuable source for tracing the evolution of her (Walker's) ideas and her art.

262. Anon. _Kirkus Reviews_ 51, No. 16 (15 August 1983): 957-958.
Interprets the essays from the viewpoint of Walker's conviction that Black writers must preserve the creations of their heritage, as well as create new awarenesses for posterity.

263. Anon. _Kliatt Young Adult Paperback Book Guide_ 19, No. 1 (January [Winter] 1985): 35.
Maintains that this volume of essays presents a direct and engrossing message from a feminist and a Black perspective.

264. Anon. _The New Yorker_ 59, No. 38 (7 November 1983): 184.
Categorizes the essays as reflections on literature, feminism, and race and evaluates her style as generally forceful and fluent.

265. Benet, Mary Kathleen. "Life-Saving Models." _Times Lit-_

erary Supplement (20 July 1984): 818.

Praises Walker as the most significant recent addition to the rising generation of Black American women writers. Contends that while the early essays sometimes sink into banality, the later autobiographical pieces display her consummate artistic skill.

266. Brown, Beth. College Language Association Journal 27, No. 3 (March 1984): 348-352.

Focuses on Walker's efforts to reconcile her responsibilities as a mother and as a writer and on her self-perceived linkage to the finest traditions of Southern literary writers: O'Connor, Faulkner, McCullers, Welty, and Hurston.

267. Chernaik, Judith. "Accidents of Birth." New Society 68, No. 1124 (7 June 1984): 393.

Contends that Walker's view of the strong, loving woman and the weak, self-centered man is unrealistic when it is applied to twentieth century British or American society.

268. Clark, Beverly Lyon. Modern Fiction Studies 30, No. 2 (Summer 1984): 334.

Lauds Walker's keen sensitivity in sifting the personal incident to reveal the universal experience. Describes the essays as "a pilgrimage in quest of the past, to redeem the past for the present."

269. Davidon, Ann Morrissett. "Beacons." Progressive 48, No. 2 (February 1984): 42-43.
Uses In Search of Our Mothers' Gardens and Outrageous Acts and Everyday Rebellions as vehicles for a comparison of the artistic perspectives shared by Walker and Gloria Steinem. Argues that the humanitarian concerns of these feminist (womanist) writers are directed toward the family of mankind.

270. Eder, Richard. Los Angeles Times Book Review (4 December 1983): 1.
Recalls some of Walker's early background as it is reflected in this volume and declares that the best writing arises from the "complex interweavings of observation, conversation, and reflection."

271. Finn, James. "Alice Walker & Flight 007: Personal Perspective: 2." Christianity and Crisis 43, No. 17 (31 October 1983): 397-398.
Critiques the essay on Flannery O'Connor and contends that Walker uses her racial heritage in a rare and successful effort to illuminate O'Connor's substantial artistic achievement.

272. Harding, William Harry. Westways 76 (January 1984): 68-

69.
Considers these essays as a historical tribute to women artists who flourished in spite of the social biases and persecutions. Praises Walker's personal essays, as opposed to the political writings, as "precisely crafted,. . . a joy to read."

273. Makowski, Elizabeth. "Women and Role Models." North American Review 270, No. 2 (June 1985): 60-61.
Recalls the author's first experience with Virginia Woolf and reveals that she could not identify with Woolf's life. Praises In Search of Our Mothers' Gardens for its success in recapturing and reevaluating the experiences of women who have led "infinitely obscure lives."

274. Mort, Mary-Ellen. Library Journal 108, No. 19 (1 November 1983): 2086.
Recommends this collection of essays which reflect Walker's civil-rights and feminist ("womanist") acttivities. Considers Walker's volume a successful redefinition of the mundane experience, viewed from her own perspective.

275. Mort, Jo-Ann. "A Prose of Her Own." Commonweal 111, No. 11 (1 June 1984): 345.
Finds this collection, generally, to be refreshing

encouragement for writers (and women writers) who must operate in a sometimes hostile environment.

276. Munro, S. Lynn. Black American Literature Forum 18, No. 4 (Winter 1984): 161.
Focuses on Walker's "humanism and her critical acumen," as well as diversity of topics which reflect her potential for personal growth and development.

277. Okri, Ben. "Colouring Book. New Statesman 107, No. 2779 (22 June 1984): 24.
Views these essays as protestations of violence against women and discrimination against Blacks and other minorities.

278. Parini, Jay. "Blowing Through the Ram's Horn: Berry, Ozick, and Others." New England Review and Bread Loaf Quarterly (Summer 1984): 630-638.
Discusses Walker's essays along with Wendell Berry's Standing By Words, Hayden Carruth's Working Papers: Selected Essays and Reviews, and Cynthia Ozick's Art and Ardor. Perceives Walker on a common ground with these writers because they all "urge us to re-forge the old connections between words and things."

279. Payne, James Robert. World Literature Today 59, No. 1 (Winter 1985): 101.

Attributes the importance of these essays to Walker's exploration of the themes in The Color Purple, her views of other writers, and her statements on major social and political issues. Notes that her reminiscences revolve around the "green air" image which reveals her consummate artistic skill.

280. Pennington, Dorothy. Quarterly Journal of Speech 72, No. 3 (August 1986): 341-344.
Discusses six anthologies of works by Black women which debunk many of the stereotypes commonly associated with women of their race. Concludes that Walker's work is both cultural and political and that it counsels Black women to reclaim the spiritual energy of their mothers by returning to their roots.

281. Rhodes, Jewell Parker. "'For There is no Friend Like a Sister in Calm or Stormy Weather.'" American 150, No. 7 (25 February 1984): 137-138.
Considers the volume an exploration into the experiences which promote bonding among Black women who influence the emergence of a world which is more equitable and humane.

282. Smith, Valerie A. "Creating Connections." Sewanee Review 93, No. 2 (Spring 1985): xxxi-xxxiv.
Lauds Walker's essays which reflect the complexities

of her mind and talent. Analyzes her style as a combination of the "deceptive simplicity" of her poetry and the "precise characterizations" of her fiction.

283. Stuttaford, Genevieve. _Publishers' Weekly_ 224, No. 10 (2 September 1983): 62.
Argues that these essays transcend the achievement of _The Color Purple_ because they encourage us to denounce all affronts to human dignity.

284. Vigderman, Patricia. "From Rags to Rage to Art." _The Nation_ 237, No. 20 (17 December 1983): 635ff.
Suggests that Walker's best writing is autobiographical and criticizes the loose construction of the exsays as a whole.

Horses Make A Landscape Look More Beautiful. New York: Harcourt, Brace, Jovanovitch, 1984.

285. Anon. _Kliatt Young Adult Paperback Book Guide_ 20, No. 3, (April [Spring] 1986): 31.
Describes the brevity and the simplicity of Walker's poems as well as the themes of humanitarian and global social concerns. Praises the volume as a reflection of the consistent quality of Walker's work.

286. Anon. "Private Voices." Books and Bookmen (September 1985): 19.

Laments the "anger and pathos" reflected in this volume which seem to reduce the poems, with few exceptions, to profuse, common-place expressions of emotion.

287. Anon. Publishers' Weekly 226, No. 8 (24 August 1984): 71.

Maintains that these poems, mainly, are banal reflections of an unsophisticated poet.

288. Anon. Virginia Quarterly Review 61, No. 2 (Spring 1985): 57.

Analyzes these poems as "simple lyrics" [arranged in] "short, non-metrical lines" and argues that the verses seem strained and forced.

289. Disch, Tom. "The Perils of Poesy." Book World (30 December 1984): 6.

Analyzes Walker's collection of poems along with the poetry of five other writers. Argues that poets should be held accountable as other writers are and contends that Walker has escaped this dictum by publishing racist prose for poetry.

290. Eaglen, Audrey. Voice of Youth Advocates 8 (April 1985):

70.

Lauds Walker for her piquant language, her elegant style, and her economy in conveying impressions about love, racism, and motherhood.

291. Gernes, Sonia <u>America</u> 152, No. 4 (2 February 1985): 93-94.

Links Walker to Walt Whitman in her celebration of the mundane problems which both divide and unite us. Argues that Walker's poems analyze "the conundrums of a world. . .in which there is a pervasive consciousness of 'those people' and 'us'."

292. Gilliland, Gail. "Walker's Poetic Voice." <u>New Directions for Women</u> 14 (May 1985): 21.

Advances the idea that <u>The Color Purple</u> embodies an eloquence which reflects Walker's literary voice and that this collection captures that quality only in a few poems.

293. Keefe, J. T. <u>World Literature Today</u> 60, No. 1 (Winter 1986): 118.

Views Walker as a visionary whose ideal world includes justice, equality, plenty, and love. Contends that she has magnificently addressed the issues of racial oppression and personal fulfillment.

294. Nower, Joyce. Library Journal 109, No. 17 (15 October 1984): 1949.
Argues that while some of the poems are dull, many reflect such diverse topics as humor, anger, and love and sparkle with the wit of a mature poet.

295. Rosenberg, L. M. New York Times Book Review (7 April 1985): 12.
Praises Walker for the music of her poetry, but contends that this volume, like the general quality of her work, has been overpraised.

The Color Purple. Produced by Steven Spielberg, Kathleen Kennedy, Frank Marshall, and Quincy Jones. Directed by Steven Spielberg. Written by Menno Meyjes. Released by Warner Brothers: Running time, 155 minutes; Rated PG-13.

296. Anon. "'The Color Purple' Brings New Black Stars to Screen in Shocking Story." Jet 69, No. 17 (13 January 1986): 58-61.
Condemns the plot of the story as a "soaring tear-jerker" but acknowledges the sterling performances given by Goldberg, Jackson, and Winfrey. Includes comments by Danny Glover in defense of the film's portrayal of the Black male image and the Black family.

297. Anon. "Readers' Response: Seeing Art and Life in _The Color Purple_ ." _Christian Century_ 103, No. 17 (14 May 1986): 495-497.
Reports six letters to the editor in response to William H. Williamon's review of _The Color Purple_. (See entry number 345.) Presents mixed reviews of Willimon's article ranging from "sexist," "myopic," and "arrogant," to full agreement that Spielberg was preoccupied with the commercial success of his movie.

298. Anon. "Seeing Red Over _Purple_." _People Weekly_ 25, No. 10 (10 March 1986): 102-104.
Gives a "battle report" on the controversy surrounding _The Color Purple_, including the portrayal of Black males and females and the eleven nominations made by the Academy of Motion Picture Arts and Sciences. Presents observations by film stars Danny Glover and Oprah Winfrey.

299. Anon. "Tenuous Places: 'Out of Africa' and 'The Color Purple'." _Commonweal_ 113, No. 2 (31 January 1986): 52-54.
Evaluates Spielberg's production as praiseworthy, but objects to the intrusion of manipulative elements of emotionalism produced by the music and the photography.

300. Ansen, David. "We Shall Overcome." _Newsweek_ 106, No. 27 (30 December 1985): 59-60.
Bemoans Spielberg's tendency to turn Walker's script into melodrama and Quincy Jones' sentimental scores, but acknowledges that the movie achieves credibility when Celie finally overcomes her oppression and begins her journey toward self-discovery.

301. Attanasio, Paul, "The Odds and the Oscars: Figuring the Favorites for Tomorrow Night's Awards." _Washington Post_, Section H (23 March 1986): 1.
Assesses the odds that _The Color Purple_ will win in the categories of "Best Picture," "Best Actress," and "Best Supporting Actress." Predicts that the performances will not earn an Oscar in either of the categories.

302. Blake, Richard. "Survivors." _America_ 154, No. 4 (1 February 1986): 75.
Commends Goldberg and Glover for their outstanding performances but argues that the movie is marred by sentimentality. Accuses Spielberg of infusing the story with extraordinary character transformations and incredible polarities for the purpose of resolving the conflicts in the story.

303. Boyd, Herb. _The Crisis_ 93, No. 2 (February 1986): 10 ff.

Condemns The Color Purple for degrading the Black male and undermining the Black family. Takes Walker to task for identifying the Black male as the problem and permitting the real enemy, the white man, to escape with impunity.

304. Boyum, Joy Gould. Glamour 84, No. 3 (March 1986): 235-236.
Comments on Hannah and Her Sisters, Out of Africa, and The Color Purple. Praises acting performances by Oprah Winfrey and Whoopi Goldberg and contends that Steven Spielberg has been successful in his debut as producer-director of serious drama.

305. Brown, Tony. "Tony Brown's Comments: The Color of Purple Is White." The Herald (1 January 1986): 2.
Attacks Walker, Spielberg, and Goldberg for their insensitivity to the injustices suffered by Black men in American society. Argues that the main focus in Purple is on the failure of Black men and "the denial of men like King, Mandella, and Malcolm who overcame the system's psychological warfare and produced healthy, non-incestuous, non-brutalizing relationships with women."

306. Bruning, Fred. "An American View: When E. T. Goes to Georgia." Maclean's 99, No. 12 (24 March 1986): 9.

Charges that Spielberg's production is flawed by a "surfeit of phony emotions and one-dimensional characters." Rejects the clear implication of the movie -- that America has evolved into a nation which has insured the equal rights of all its citizens.

307. Campbell, James. "The Color Rosy." _Times Literary Supplement_ (11 July 1986): 762.
Castigates Spielberg for ". . . the trivialization of a fine novel" through his sentimental approach in transforming Walker's material from book to movie. Allows modest praise for Margaret Avery and Whoopi Goldberg, who manage dignified performances.

308. Canby, Vincent. "From a Palette of Cliches Comes 'The Color Purple.'" _New York Times_ (5 January 1986): Section 2, p. 17.
Praises Goldberg and Avery for their performances, but takes Spielberg to task for making a movie which is satisfying but without "original artistic merit."

309. Champlin, Charles. "Critic at Large: Spielberg's Primary 'Color.'" _Los Angeles Times_, Part V (28 December 1985): 1.
Argues that although Spielberg's script is decidedly different from his previous ones, his technique has not changed significantly. Concludes that the story

and theme of The Color Purple place it squarely in the realm of melodrama.

310. ________. "Spielberg's Escape from Escapism." Los Angeles Times (2 February 1986): 12 ff.
Reveals biographical information about Spielberg, as well as his attitudes about film-making. Explains the reasons why he decided to film The Color Purple.

311. Collier, Aldore. "Margaret Avery Says She 'Couldn't Buy A Job' Before 'The Color Purple.'" Jet 69, No. 25 (10 March 1986): 58-60.
Describes Avery's problems in finding acting parts and explains how fate, circumstance, and determination provided the impetus for acquiring her role in The Color Purple.

312. "The Color Purple." The Christian Century 103, No. 4 (29 January 1986): 99.
Lauds Spielberg's debut as a director of serious films because of his "sentimental touch" which removes the edge of pain and suffering for the reader.

313. Corliss, Richard. "The Three Faces of Steve." Time 126, No. 25 (23 December 1985): 78.
Castigates Spielberg for his efforts to romanticize the story by minimizing the scenes of "raw artistry"

such as the separation of the sisters and the enactment of the lesbian scene. Argues that the movie comes across as "cinematography, not cinema."

314. Denby, David. "Purple People-Eater." *New York* 19, No. 2 (13 January 1986): 56-57.
Repudiates *The Color Purple* as "inauthentic" and "sentimental." Protests the portrayal of the men as innately cruel and the women as struggling saints. Rejects the acting (except for Margaret Avery) as unconvincing and misdirected.

315. Dworkin, Susan. "The Strange and Wonderful Story of the Making of 'The Color Purple.'" *Ms*. 14, No. 6 (December 1985): 66-70 ff.
Reveals Walker's decision to proceed with Quincy Jones' "social conscience," Steven Spielberg's perception of the "spirit" of the novel, and Menno Meyjes' understanding of "folk speech." Acknowledges Walker's need to have Celie's story reach beyond the reading audience to touch the lives of her theatergoing constituency.

316. Fontenot, Chester, Jr. "Even Sinners Have Souls: A Black Male's Response to 'The Color Purple.'" *The Afroamericanist Newsletter* 1, No. 3 (1986): 2-4.
Maintains that Shug's father and the transformed Al-

bert represent positive images of Black males which negate the charge that Walker's Black men are despicable and beastly. Places responsibility for Celie's dilemma on her own attitude and inability to act and concludes that the fates of Black women and Black men are inextricably bound, one to the other.

317. Gable, Mona. "Author Alice Walker Discusses 'The Color Purple.'" The Wall Street Journal 206, No. 121 (19 December 1985): 26.
Relates Walker's satisfaction with the movie because it brought the speech of the people in her community of Eatonton, Georgia back to life. (See Walker's Letter to the Editor, "The Color Purple," in the listing of "Essays and Letters.")

318. Goldstein, William. "The Story Behind the Movie: Alice Walker on the Set of 'The Color Purple.'" Publishers' Weekly 228, No. 10 (6 September 1985): 46-48.
Describes Walker's involvement in selecting the casting and the props used in the movie. Explains the artistic stances taken by director Steven Spielberg and screenwriter Menno Meyjes as they worked in close collaboration with Walker.

319. Hey, Kenneth R. "The Color Purple." USA Today 114, No. 2490 (March 1986): 92-93.

Provides a succinct contrast between the art of producer Steven Spielberg and writer Alice Walker. Concludes that Walker's reality and Spielberg's fantasy emerge as incongruous, irreconcilable elements.

320. Keal, Pauline. "Sacred Monsters." _The New Yorker_ 61, No. 45 (30 December 1985): 67-71.

Reviews _The Color Purple_ along with two other current films. Bemoans Walker's female chauvinism, Spielberg's failure to capture Walker's "earthy folk style," Quincy Jones' "gooey" score, Menno Meyjes' ineffective script, and (except for Oprah Winfrey), the lukewarm acting by the cast.

321. Kauffmann, Stanley. "Sign of the Times." _The New Republic_ 194, No. 4 (27 January 1986): 24-25.

Traces briefly the history of films made about Blacks and contends that the _The Color Purple_ is successful because of Spielberg's abilty to assess his audience and release a mass-appeal film on Black life with precision timing and because of his conviction that happy endings are essential in the world of filmmaking.

322. Kehr, Dave. "Call of the Wild." _American Film_ 12, No. 3 (December 1986): 43-46ff.

Traces the theme of primitivism in the movies to

Rudyard Kipling, Henry Rider Haggar, and Arthur Conan Doyle, whose works are based on the assumption that triumphant whites are the heroes, while African natives are unschooled and uncivilized. Views *The Color Purple* from the perspective of sex as the catalyst which propels Celie from the "paradise of childhood" into the unglamorous world of adult responsibility.

323. Kennedy, Harlan. "Amazon Grace." *Film Comment* 22, No. 5 (September/October 1986): 9-15.
Advances the theory that although many current movies depict Indians and Blacks, they function as emblems and symbols who never lay claim to their full humanity. Examines *The Color Purple*, *The Emerald Forest*, *Out of Africa*, *The Mission*, and *Greystroke* from this perspective.

324. Kopkind, Andrew. "The Color Purple." *The Nation* (1 February 1986): 124-125.
Compares the movie with other current productions and concludes that the film has great popular appeal because it presents us with a counter-cultural realism which challenges our concepts of the Great American Dream.

325. Mars-Jones, Adam. "Mauve." *New Statesman* 112, No. 2885

(11 July 1986): 27-28.
Advances the idea that the melodramatic plot and the narrative of the novel constitute serious structural defects which Spielberg was unable to conceal in the screen adaptation.

326. Mathews, Jack. "Spielberg's Loss Now Makes Him Talk of the Town." _Los Angeles Times_, Part 6 (7 February 1986): 1.
Comments on the pros and cons of Spielberg's failure to garner the "Best Director" award for _The Color Purple_, in spite of the eleven other nominations for an Oscar and the $40 million box-office receipts.

327. ____________. "3 'Color Purple' Actresses Talk About Its Impact." _Los Angeles Times_, Part VI (31 January 1986): 1 ff.
Focuses on the popular and critical receptions given the movie, as well as the personal satisfaction derived from telling Celie's story.

328. McCaffery, Larry. _Los Angeles Times Book Review_ (20 April 1986): 15.
Reviews Ishmael Reed's novel, _Reckless Eyeballing_, and joins Reed in his condemnation of what McCaffery refers to as the "deodorized banalities" of _The Color_

Purple.

329. McGuigan, Cathleen. "Whoopee for Whoopi." *Newsweek* 106, No. 27 (30 December 1985): 60.
Traces Goldberg's success from a small West Coast theater in 1982 to her flawless performance, which gives *The Color Purple* its "center of gravity."

330. Moore, Trudy S. "Danny Glover: Villain in 'Color Purple' Is a Kind Family Man." *Jet* 69, No. 26 (17 March 1986): 28-31.
Contrasts Glover in his role as a hostile, insensitive, abusive husband in *The Color Purple* with his presence in real life as a caring, attentive husband and father.

331. Neven, Tom. "'Even Sinners Have Souls.'" *Christianity Today* 30, No. 4 (7 March 1986): 59-60.
Interprets the message of the movie as an assurance that the grace of God prevails in this world as well as in the next. Praises Spielberg for the manifestations of God's grace which are revealed throughout the movie.

332. Norment, Lynn. "The Color Purple." *Ebony* 41, No. 4 (February 1986): 146 ff.
Acknowledges the commendable performances of the

cast and the significant achievements of Steven Spielberg and Quincy Jones, but criticizes the lack of positive Black characters -- male and female -- and calls for more movies, backed by the same resources and talent, to "celebrate the positive aspects of Black America."

333. Pally, Marcia. "Women in Love." Film Comment 22, No. 2 (April 1986): 35-39.
Identifies current sociological problems encountered by filmmakers in depicting lesbianism on the screen. Castigates Steven Spielberg for emphasizing familial bonds at the expense of sexual intimacy, especially where Celie and Shug are involved.

334. Pinckney, Darryl. "Black Victims, Black Villains." New York Review of Books 34, No. 1 (29 January 1987): 17-20.
Acknowledges Walker's intentions to glorify Africa and Blackness via the inspiration she found in the writings of Zora Neale Hurston. Contends, however, that The Color Purple more nearly establishes Walker's kinship with Harriet Beecher Stowe and Uncle Tom's Cabin. Compares the movie with The Birth of A Nation and excoriates Walker for allowing Speilberg to ignore the rampant poverty which existed

for Blacks during the depression and for translating the brutality of whites toward all Blacks into a general misapprehension that the Black man is the enemy of the Black woman. Cites Ishmael Reed's Reckless Eyeballing as a refutation of these historical inaccuracies and praises Reed as "one of the most underrated writers in America."

335. Robertson, Nan. "Actresses' Varied Roads to 'The Color Purple.'" New York Times, Section C (13 February 1986): 21.
Discusses the different professional backgrounds of the four actresses who star in The Color Purple and their zest and enthusiasm for the opportunities and challenges presented by the script.

336. Rothenstein, Richard. "The Color Film." Saturday Review 12, No. 3 (May/June 1986): 79.
Analyzes the prolific use of names of colors in recent film titles. Contends that the color "purple" suggests spirituality and intensity of feeling.

337. Salaam, Kalamu ya. "The Color Purple: Watered Down or Brightened Up?" The New Orleans Tribune (January 1986): 24-25.
Contends that Walker's novel is a significant presentation of "hardcore truths," but Spielberg fails

to translate this vision to the screen. Argues that the movie skirts the serious issues and reduces Walker's "lion" to a domesticated beast whose temperament is compatible with the "lamb."

338. Salamon, Julie. "...As Spielberg's Film Version Is Released." The Wall Street Journal 206, No. 121 (19 December 1985): 6.
Bemoans the fact that Spielberg fails to translate the suffering, the hostility, and the bitterness of Walker's novel onto the screen. Contends that the decision to minimize the intensity of Shug's and Celie's relationship undermined the potential dramatic impact of the movie.

339. Seitz, Michael H. "Pop Purple." The Progressive 50, No. 2 (February 1986): 40.
Bemoans Spielberg's efforts to render Walker's novel powerless by "deleting, diluting, or sanitizing" such significant themes as male violence, brutalization racism, sexism, religious hypocrisy, lesbianism, female sexual independence, and colonial exploitation.

340. Silverman, Marjorie Saxon. "Dutch Scripter Found Universality of People Key to 'Purple' Project." Variety 322, No. 7 (12 March 1986): 18.

Comments on the harmonious collaboration between producer Steven Spielberg and scriptwriter Menno Meyjes, who defends the character portrayals as authentic and universal.

341. Simon, John. "Black and White in Purple." _National Review_ 38, No. 2 (14 February 1986): 56-59.
Analyzes _The Color Purple_ and _Out of Africa_ as contemporary films. Contends that Steven Spielberg reduced Walker's overrated novel to "an infantile abomination."

342. Travers, Peter. _People Weekly_ (6 January 1986): 18.
Castigates Spielberg for transforming poverty, incest, racism, rape, and lesbianism into a fairy tale. Finds Quincy Jones' musical score "obtrusive" and Danny Glover's character change unbelievable. Praises Oprah Winfrey and Whoopi Goldberg, whose performances "give the movie a sense of pride that is the film's final glory."

343. Trescott, Jacqueline. "Passions Over 'Purple.'" _Washington Post_, Section C (3 February 1986): 1.
Discusses how some Black men view _The Color Purple_ and how it depicts negative attitudes in Black female/male relationships. Argues that the brutalization of Black women by Black men is not a realistic

picture of Black America.

344. Wesley, Richard. "'The Color Purple' Debate." *Ms.* 15, No. 3 (September 1986): 62 ff.
Contends that, as a writer, Walker serves as an "antenna" of society, and therefore, her views should not be censured. Asserts that while *The Color Purple* does not include positive male images, many Black male writers in the 1950's and 1960's who projected negative female images escaped condemnation. Concludes that the real villains are whites who control the production of books, plays, and movies about Blacks and prevent consideration of Walker's writings within a broader context.

345. Willimon, William H. "Seeing Red Over 'The Color Purple.'" *Christian Century* 103, No. 11 (2 April 1986): 319.
Praises "two [unnamed] extremely talented Black actresses" for their performances but castigates Spielberg for his "cinematic cliches" and his penchant for substituting stereotypes for realistic characters. (See entry number 297.)

346. Willis, John. "The Color Purple." In his *Screen World*, Volume 37. *New York*: Crown Publishers, Incorporated, 1986, pp. 94-95.

Lists full cast and credits, as well as illustrations of scenes from Steven Spielberg's production of _The Color Purple_.

Articles and Essays

347. Baker, Houston A. Jr. and Charlotte Pierce-Baker. "Patches: Quilts and Community in Alice Walker's 'Everyday Use.'" _The Southern Review_ 21, No. 3 (July 1985): 706-720.

Views Walker's short story, "Everyday Use," as an introduction to _The Color Purple_ and a testimony to her conviction that function is superior to art in the "fiction of sacred creation." Argues that quiltmaking is "the signal mode of confronting chaos through a skillful blending of patches."

348. Buncombe, Marie H. "Androgyny as Metaphor in Alice Walker's Novels." _College Language Association Journal_ 30, No. 4 (June 1987): 419-427.

Contends that androgyny symbolizes "wholeness" for Walker. Therefore, her characters achieve self-actualization as they recognize and accept the best characteristics within themselves without consideration for social stereotypes associated with gender or sex.

349. Christian, Barbara. "Alice Walker: The Black Woman Artist As Wayward." _Black Women Writers (1950-1980): A Critical Evaluation_. Edited by Mari Evans. Garden City, New York: Anchor Press/Doubleday, 1984, pp. 457-477.

Examines Walker's recurrent themes and characterizes her writings as "a process of stripping off layers, honing down to the core." Contends that love of self, as a prerequisite for self-fulfillment, is linked to the ability to be honest about the realities of life and the commitment to challenge those realities from within as well as from without.

350. ___________. "The Contrary Women of Alice Walker." _The Black Scholar_ 12, No. 2 (March-April 1981): 21 ff.

Probes the attitudes held by whites and Blacks concerning the role of the Black woman. Concludes that the stories in _In Love and Trouble_ "are about the most natural law of all, that living beings must love themselves, must try to be free -- that spirit will eventually triumph over convention, no matter what the cost."

351. ___________. "Novels for Everyday Use: The Novels of Alice Walker." In her _Black Women Novelists: The Development of a Tradition, 1892-1976_. Westport,

Connecticut: Greenwood Press, 1980, pp. 180-238. Concentrates on The Third Life of Grange Copeland and Meridian as novels based upon the themes of perceptions of the past and recognition of the element of struggle as vital concepts in the search for personal transformation in the present and regeneration in the future.

352. Coleman, Viralene J. "Miss Celie's Song." Publication of the Arkansas Philological Association 11 (Spring 1985): 27-34.
Characterizes Celie as a sanguine, forbearing individual whose personal growth and development evolve as a result of her flexible nature and her capacity for love and forgiveness.

353. Cooke, Michael. "Intimacy: The Interpenetration of the One and the All in Robert Hayden and Alice Walker." In his Afro-American Literature in the Twentieth Century: The Achievement of Intimacy. New Haven: Yale University Press, 1984, pp. 133-176.
Focuses on Walker's Meridian as a repudiation of the conventional expressions of intimacy (such as sex) and as "a summons to an inimitable intimacy for a reluctant world."

354. Davis, Thadious M. "Alice Walker's Celebration of Self

in Southern Generations." _Women Writers of the Contemporary South_. Edited by Peggy Whitman Prensaw. Jackson: University Press of Mississippi, 1984, pp. 38-53.

Presents a summary of Walker's artistic philosophy which is grounded in dual Black and Southern heritages. Refers to specific works that illustrate her major themes and suggests reasons why readers find her messages so compelling.

355. El Saffar, Ruth. "Alice Walker's _The Color Purple_." _The International Fiction Review_ 12, No. 1 (Winter 1985): 11-17.

Views the novel as a journey toward self-discovery undertaken by two sisters who come to understand that God is an internal rather than an external force.

356. Erikson, Peter. "Cast Out Alone/To Heal/And Re-Create/ Ourselves: Family-Based Identity in the Work of Alice Walker." _College Language Association Journal_ 23, No. 1 (September 1979): 71-94.

Explores intra-family relationships in _The Third Life of Grange Copeland_, "A Sudden Trip Home in the Spring," and _Meridian_. Focuses on the premise that family background must be utilized as a resource and strength, rather than a burden or liability.

357. Fifer, Elizabeth. "The Dialect and Letters of The Color Purple." Contemporary American Women Writers. Edited by Catherine Rainwater and W. J. Scheick. Lexington, Kentucky: University Press of Kentucky, 1985, pp. 155-165.
Lauds Walker's deft use of narration which contrasts Celie's folk language with Nettie's polished diction and leads us into an understanding of and appreciation for Celie's predicament "within a larger cultural context."

358. Fishman, Charles. "Naming Names: Three Recent Novels By Women Writers." Names 32, No. 1 (March 1984): 33-44.
Discusses the use of names to suggest levels and boundaries, status, mis-naming, power, and roots in Walker's Meridian, Margaret Atwood's Life Before Man, and Toni Morrison's Tar Baby.

359. Fontenot, Chester J. "Alice Walker: 'The Diary of An African Nun' and DuBois' Double Consciousness." Sturdy Black Bridges: Visions of Black Women in Literature. Edited by Roseann P. Bell, Bettye J. Parker, and Beverly Guy-Sheftall. New York: Anchor Press/Doubleday, 1979, pp. 150-156 (Selected bibliography, pp. 402-403.)

Focuses on the allegorical significance of the short story and interprets the African nun as the Black intellectual or middle class, a victim of DuBois' "double consciousness, ...caught between two worlds which are at once complementary and contradictory."

360. Freeman, Alice S. "Zora Neale Hurston and Alice Walker: A Spiritual Kinship." Sage 2, No. 1 (Spring 1985): 37-40.
Compares Hurston's Janie Crawford (Their Eyes Were Watching God) with three of Walker's female characters. Concludes that Hurston and Walker both share a "bond of kinship" which evolves out of their mutual commitment to analyze the rich heritage of Black women in the United States.

361. Friend, Beverly Oberfield. "Popular Culture." The Women's Annual: 1982-83. Edited by Barbara Haber. Boston: G. K. Hall and Company, 1983, pp. 149-176.
Discusses the heroines in recent movies and novels. Critiques The Color Purple by focusing on the bonding of females which makes Celie's survival possible.

362. Gaston, Karen C. "Women in the Lives of Grange Copeland." College Language Association Journal 24, No. 3 (March 1981): 276-286.

Advances the argument that the women in _The Third Life of Grange Copeland_ frequently extend their love at the expense of exerting their obvious strength. On the other hand, the irresponsible men use their power to crush and kill the objects of their love.

363. Harris, Trudier. "Folklore in the Fiction of Alice Walker: A Perpetuation of Historical and Literary Traditions." _Black American Literature Forum_ 11, No. 1 (Spring 1977): 3-8.
Argues that Walker draws on the literary traditions of Chesnutt, Hurston, and Toomer in "The Revenge of Hannah Kemhuff" and _The Third Life of Grange Copeland_ to develop characters, illuminate their interrelationships, and condemn negative attitudes shared by Blacks toward each other. Maintains that Walker also uses folklore to make direct criticism of racial discrimination in the United States.

364. ___________. "From Victimization to Free Enterprise: Alice Walker's _The Color Purple_." _Studies in American Fiction_ 14, No. 1 (Spring 1986): 1-17.
Compares selected women characters from Walker's earlier works with Celie in _The Color Purple_. Concludes that Celie's transformation near the end of the novel is unrealistic and that she represents a

reincarnation of old stereotypes, rather than the emergence of self-affirmation as a point of progression for the Black woman.

365. ___________. "On _The Color Purple_, Stereotypes and Silence." _Black American Literature Forum_ 18, No. 4 (Winter 1984): 155-161.
Contends that _The Color Purple_ propagates common myths of sex and violence held by whites about Blacks. Objects to the negative portrayal of Black men and argues that the depiction of Black women is also unrealistic.

366. ___________. "Three Black Women Writers and Humanism: A Folk Perspective." _Black American Literature and Humanism_. Edited by R. Baxter Miller. Lexington, Kentucky: University Press of Kentucky, 1981, pp. 50-74.
Examines Grange Copeland's philosophy of life, along with a consideration of characters created by Sara Wright and Paule Marshall. Argues that folk culture, not religion, functions as the basis for the humanism which governs the lives of these people.

367. ___________. "Tiptoeing Through Taboo: Incest in 'The Child Who Favored Daughter.'" _Modern Fiction Studies_ 28, No. 3 (Autumn 1982): 495-505.

Advances the argument that Walker has joined the few other Black writers who have ventured to discuss the virtually taboo subject of incest. However, her use of symbolism and her implicit development do not represent a significant departure from the norm.

368. __________. "Violence in The Third Life of Grange Copeland." _College Language Association Journal_ 19, No. 2 (December 1975): 238-247.
Analyzes black-on-black violence through the characters of Grange and Brownfield Copeland. Concludes that Grange accepts moral responsibility for his actions and that the violence which he perpetrates is "a necessary evil to destroy evil." Brownfield's hostility, on the other hand, motivates him to commit wanton violent acts which are directed toward his family.

369. Hellenbrand, Harold. "Speech After Silence: Alice Walker's _The Third Life of Grange Copeland_." _Black American Literature Forum_ 20, Nos. 1-2 (Spring-Summer 1986): 113-128.
Views Walker's novel as a saga of a Black family whose power to love is nearly destroyed by conflicts which they experience in a white-dominated society. Advances the argument that "the novel points toward

the reconstitution of female identity and family life."

370. Henderson, Mae G. "The Color Purple: Revisions and Redefinitions." Sage 2, No. 1 (Spring 1985): 14-18. Recognizes that Walker has broken new ground in converting the epistolary novel from a medium of male dominance to a vehicle which promotes the concept of female bonding. Concludes that the novel progresses from the subjugation of male-female relationships to the equality of female/female ties and, finally, to a "female/male/female triad based on new and redefined roles."

371. Krauth, Leland. "Mark Twain, Alice Walker, and the Aesthetics of Joy." Proteus (Fall 1984): 9-14. Compares Huckleberry Finn and The Color Purple and concludes that both novels present themes of violence, suffering, isolation, cruelty, and injustice. Both novels celebrate the triumph of the self over the sinister forces which jeopardize its existence, and both view God as the human potential for goodness, thus giving rise to a moral force which creates hope and joy.

372. McDowell, Deborah E. "The Self in Bloom: Alice Walker's Meridian." College Language Association Journal 24,

No. 3 (March 1981): 262-275.
Views the novel from a universal perspective which involves the concerns of self-determination and self-actualization. Classifies the story as a _Bildungs-roman_ which begins with a series of initiatory experiences and ends in the achievement of Meridian's "psychic wholeness."

373. McGowan, Martha J. "Atonement and Release in Alice Walker's _Meridian_." _Critique_ 23, No. 1 (Fall 1981-82): 25-36.
Views the novel as a continuation of the theme of morality and ethics which Walker began in _The Third Life of Grange Copeland_. Compares Meridian to Camus' rebel and argues that Walker has acknowledged the belief that rebellion may involve guilt and atonement.

374. Mickleson, Anne Z. "Winging Upward: Black Women: Sara E. Wright, Toni Morrison, Alice Walker." In her _Reaching Out: Sensitivity and Order in Recent American Fiction By Women_. Metuchen, New Jersey: The Scarecrow Press, Inc. 1979, pp. 112-174.
Interprets the internal and external motivations operating in the lives of the women in _In Love and Trouble_, _Meridian_, and selected works of Sara E.

Wright and Toni Morrison. Praises Walker for the verisimilitude in her writing and her use of myth, dialect, and the "vivid, metaphorical language of Black people."

375. Nadelhaft, Ruth. "Domestic Violence in Literature: A Preliminary Study." Mosaic 17, No. 2 (Spring 1984: 242-259.
Begins with Othello and examines domestic violence in several other selected works, including The Color Purple, which presents a unique solution. Although Henry James (The Sacred Fount) argued that one person acquires power at the expense of the other, Walker provides for a redistribution of domestic power which results in the achievement of peace and tranquility in the domestic relationship.

376. Nowak, Hanna. "Alice Walker: Poetry Celebrating Life." A Salzburg Miscellany: English and American Studies, 1964-1984. Edited by Wilfried Haslauer. Salzburg: University of Salzburg Press, 1984, pp. 111-125.
Categorizes Walker's poems as ones which concern the history of Black people, the intimate, personal love experience, and the public poems which reflect her "womanist" views. Argues, contrary to dominant critical views, that Walker is a better poet than a

fiction writer.

377. Nowik, Nan. "Mixing Art and Politics: The Writing of Adrienne Rich, Marge Piercy, and Alice Walker.: *The Centennial Review* 30, No. 2 (Spring 1986): 208-218. Analyzes the academic backgrounds of Rich, Piercy, and Walker to determine how they progressed from the viewpoint of their mentors that art and politics must be separate and arrived at the recognition that art and politics are inseparable.

378. Parker-Smith, Bettye J. "Alice Walker's Women: In Search of Some Peace of Mind." *Black Women Writers (1950-1980): A Critical Evaluation*. Edited by Mari Evans. Garden City, New York: Anchor Press/Doubleday, 1984. pp. 478-493.
Comments on Walker's use of the South as a "spiritual balance and an ideological base" from which she depicts the evolution of the emergent woman, symbolized first by Ruth (*The Third Life of Grange Copeland*), Meridian, in the novel of the same title, and Celie in *The Color Purple*, which "elevates Black women to the height of sovereignty."

379. Peden, William. "The Black Explosion: 'I Mean, With All Things Considered, The Field Is Opening Up More and More . . . Ya Know--Bein' Black and Meanin' It.

We're in Vogue These Days.'" In his The American Short Story: Continuity and Change, 1940-1975. Boston: Houghton-Mifflin Company, 1975, pp. 134-147. Praises In Love and Trouble as the work of a disciplined, major writer who maintains consummate control over her material. Contends that both Walker and Ernest Gaines have been successful in elevating their prose beyond sociology to the dominion of art.

380. Sadoff, Dianne F. "Black Matrilineage: The Case of Alice Walker and Zora Neale Hurston." Signs II, No. 1 (Autumn 1985): 4-26.
Argues that the modern female Black writer has an obligation to recapture lost culture and history and that recognition of her "literary maternity" is a prerequisite toward that end. Uses this theory to explain Walker's acknowledgment of her literary debt to Zora Neale Hurston, whose work is regarded as archetypal. Contends that Hurston and Walker have essentially the same message: women's relationships with men impede their achievement of self-actualization.

381. Shelton, Frank W. "Alienation and Integration in Alice Walker's The Color Purple." College Language Association Journal 28, No. 4 (June 1985): 382-392.

Focuses on the relationships between men and women, among women, between people and nature, and between people and God. Contends that male aggression and hostility prevent communication between the sexes and that this contact becomes possible only when males and females achieve a sense of dignity and self-worth.

382. Stade, George. "Womanist Fiction and Male Characters." _Partisan Review_ 52, No. 3 (1985): 264-270.
Distinguishes between feminism, which promotes equality of the sexes, and womanism, which demonstrates the superiority of virtuous women over depraved men. Provides historical precedent for Walker's womanism and argues that _The Color Purple_ is informed by a "female chauvinism," a "narcissistic rage" which depicts men as monsters without ever explaining why they are so degenerate.

383. Stein, Karen F. "Meridian: Alice Walker's Critique of Revolution." _Black American Literature Forum_ 20, Nos. 1-2 (Spring-Summer 1986): 129-141.
Analyzes _Meridian_ as a work which rejects those basic social tenets that deny the selfhood of women. Contends that the novel extols the virtues of life over death, a victory which is achieved only through the

painstaking examination of the self.

384. Walker, Robbie. "Coping Strategies of the Women in Alice Walker's Novels: Implications for Survival." _College Language Association Journal_ 30, No. 4 (June 1987): 401-418.

Analyzes the strategies for coping with the circumstances of their environment which are used by selected female characters created by Walker. Concludes that the formulation of a successful strategy is contingent upon a clear recognition by these women that they are in control of their own lives.

385. Washington, Mary Helen. "An Essay on Alice Walker." _Sturdy Black Bridges: Visions of Black Women in Literature_, Edited by Roseann P. Bell, Bettye J. Parker, and Beverly Guy-Sheftall. New York: Anchor Press/Doubleday 1979, pp. 133-149. (Selected bibliography, pp. 402-403.)

Comments on internal and external forces operating in the lives of Black women and analyzes their experiences in terms of historical cycles: the suspended woman of the eighteenth, nineteenth, and early twentieth centuries, the assimilated woman of the late '40's and '50's, and the emergent woman of the late '60's.

386. ______. "Teaching Black-Eyed Susans: An Approach to the Study of Black Women Writers." _Black American Literature Forum_ 11, No. 1 (Spring 1977): 20-24.

Suggests that the works of Walker and several other Black women writers might be studied through thematic and historical approaches. Subdivides the historical approach into "The Suspended Woman," "The Assimilated Woman," and "The Emergent Woman," and suggests characters and works which fit into these categories.

387. White, Vernessa C. _"The Third Life of Grange Copeland_ and _Meridian_: The Southern Experience and Evolution of Black American Consciousness." In her _Afro-American and East German Fiction: A Comparative Study of Alienation, Identity, and the Development of Self_. New York: Peter Land Publishers, Inc. 1983, pp. 91-115.

Regards _Meridian_ as a continuation of _The Third Life of Grange Copeland_. Compares Walker's novels with those of Toni Morrison because of their "authentic depiction of the horrors which blight the lives of some black Americans."

388. Willis, Susan. "Alice Walker's Women." _New Orleans_

Review 12, No. 1 (Spring 1985): 33-41.

Advances the theory that Walker uses the anecdotal narrative to avoid the chauvinistic literary canons advanced by Richard Wright and develop a "viable literary language." Observes that Walker's women represent the peasant underclass whose liberation is crucial to the "radical transformation of society."

389. Worthington, Pepper. "Writing a Rationale for a Controversial Common Reading Book: Alice Walker's The Color Purple." English Journal 74, No. 1 (January 1985): 48-52.

Isolates four controversial issues in Walker's novel: subject matter, language, grammar, and form. Attempts to answer these objections for the high school English teacher who is confronted with problems of censorship.

Miscellany

390. Anon. "Alice Walker: Going Her Own Way." Vanity Fair 46 (April 1983): 90-91.

Discusses Walker briefly as a unique artistic voice who has given expression to womens' experiences as they seek to preserve discarded remnants of Black culture.

391. Anon. "Alice Walker Addresses Students Via TV Hookup." Jet 71, No. 13 (15 December 1986): 60.
Summarizes briefly the details of Walker's two-hour program, "A Private Conversation With Alice Walker," which was broadcast via closed circuit television and viewed by students on 100 college campuses.

392. Anon. "Alice Walker Goes Home to Eatonton, Ga. for 'Color Purple' Premiere." Jet 69, No. 21 (10 February 1986): 28-30.
Recalls the festivities and accolades surrounding Walker's return to her hometown in Eatonton for the premiere of The Color Purple.

393. Anon. "Author Alice Walker Wins Pulitzer Prize for Novel." Jet 64, No. 9 (9 May 1983): 9.
Announces Walker as the first Black woman to win the Pulitzer Prize for fiction. Gives very brief biographical and bibliographical data.

394. Anon. "The Creative Woman Requires Talent and Drive." Ebony 32, No. 10 (August 1977): 135.
Spotlights Alice Walker (along with several other Black women) and her achievements as writer and artist.

395. Anon. "Goldberg, Avery, Winfrey Up for Oscars in 'Pur-

ple'." _Jet_ 69, No. 23 (24 February 1986): 54.
Announces Oscar nominations for Whoopi Goldberg, Margaret Avery, and Oprah Winfrey in the "Best Actress" and "Best Supporting Actress" categories for their roles in _The Color Purple_.

396. Anon. "Hollywood NAACP Scolds Academy Award Execs for 'Color Purple' Shut Out." _Jet_ 70, No. 4 (14 April 1986): 52-53.
Reports contents of a letter from the President of the Hollywood/Beverly Hills Branch of the NAACP. Willis Edwards accuses the Academy's Board of Governors of racism after the movie failed to win a single Oscar, in spite of the eleven nominations that it received.

397. Anon. "The Legacy of Phillis Wheatley." _Ebony_ 29, No. 5 (March 1974): 94 ff.
Features Walker as one of eighteen Black women poets assembled at Jackson State University to honor the genius of Phillis Wheatley.

398. Anon. "Making Change." _Ms_. 14, No. 2 (August 1985): 68.
Announces Walker's establishment of Wild Trees Press, whose goal is to remain small and publish a few of the "manuscripts we love and can't bear not to have available."

399. Anon. "1985 Academy Award Nominations." _Variety_ 322, No. 3 (12 February 1986): 4ff.
Gives complete categorical listings of all Academy Award nominations for pictures released in 1985.

400. Anon. "NOW Honors Oprah Winfrey for 'Color Purple' Role." _Jet_ 70, No. 15 (30 June 1986): 29.
Reports Oprah Winfrey's selection by the National Organization for Women (NOW) for the Women of Achievement Award, based on her role in _The Color Purple_.

401. Anon. "An Unknown Actress's Advertising Campaign Draws Ire." _People Weekly_ 25, No. 10 (10 March 1986): 104ff.
Alleges that a full-page advertisement taken out by Margaret Avery in _The Hollywood Reporter_ was intended to exploit her role in _The Color Purple_ and influence the Academy of Motion Picture Arts and Sciences to pass favorably on her nomination in the category of "Best Supporting Actress."

402. Anon. "Whoopi's Blue Eyes." _Harper's Magazine_ 274, No. 1640 (January 1987): 29.
Excerpts comments made by Spike Lee in an interview with Marlaine Glicksman (See entry number 408).
Focuses on Lee's comments on _The Color Purple_ and

his allegation that Walker intended for her film to appeal to whites and their stereotypical ideas about the Black male.

403. Bailey, Carl. "Eye on Publishing." _Wilson Library Bulletin_ 57, No. 10 (June 1983): 844-845.
Describes The American Book Awards (TABA) for 1982 and comments briefly on Walker's selection in the category of "hardcover fiction" for _The Color Purple_.

404. Baker, John F. "TABA Tries the Library: Fourth Awards Blossom in a Bookish Setting." _Publishers' Weekly_ 223, No. 19 (13 May 1983): 16-17.
Quotes comments made by Walker in her acceptance speech for the American Book Award for fiction at the New York Public Library, April 28, 1983.

405. Bass, Carole and Paul Bass. "Censorship American Style." _Index on Censorship_ 14 (1985): 6-7.
Summarizes key presentations at a writers conference on censorship sponsored by the National Writers Union. Synopsizes Alice Walker's opening night speech which details her experiences with the censorship of the Black folk language in _The Color Purple_.

406. Benfey, Christopher. _New York Times_ (27 April 1986): Section 7, p. 22.

Reviews the 66th O. Henry Award prize stories and contends that Walker's "Kindred Spirits" justly deserves first place among them.

407. Clarke, Gerald. "Suprise! An Oscar Entertains: 'Out of Africa' is in and 'The Color Purple' is Blue." _Time_ 127, No. 14 (7 April 1986): 83.
Argues that the unpredictability of the awards for 1986 infused the program with a suspense and entertainment which was atypical of previous ceremonies. Mentions the fact that _The Color Purple_ won no awards but contends that other movies, despite their multiple nominations, have also shared the same fate.

408. Glicksman, Marlaine. "Lee Way." _Film Comment_ 22, No. 5 September/October 1986): 46-49.
Presents an interview with Spike Lee, director and producer of _She's Gotta Have It_, who explains the problems associated with making a low-budget film. Lee compares his film with _The Color Purple_ and alleges that Alice Walker's unjustified denigration of Black men influenced whites to award her the Pulitzer Prize and to make a film based on the novel. Criticizes the work of Ntozake Shange, also, for her portrayal of one-dimensional males but praises Toni Morrison for her positive approach toward the depic-

tion of the Black male. (See entry number 402.)

409. Graham, Keith. "Three to Get Smith Writing Awards." _Atlanta Consitution_, Section D (14 November 1984): 6.
Announces Alice Walker, John Egerton, and Eudora Welty as the Lillian Smith Award recipients for 1984.

410. Grimm, Fred. "'Color Purple' Author Receives Joyous Welcome." _Miami Herald_, Section A (19 January 1986): 1ff.
Recounts the jubilation in Eatonton and the spirit of cooperation among whites and Blacks as Walker returns home for the premiere of _The Color Purple_ and the reception held in her honor.

411. "Let Us Now Praise Unsung Writers." _Mother Jones_ 11, No. 1 (January 1986): 27-28.
Reports on a _Mother Jones_ survey of selected American writers to determine their favorite foreign writers who deserve more attention from American readers and critics. Summarizes Walker's comments on her choices: Bessie Head, Camara Laye, and Ayi Kwei Armah.

412. McCarthy, Todd. "'Purple,' 'Africa' Pace Academy Nods with 11 Apiece; Spielberg Shut Out, Indies Show Up Strong." _Variety_ 322, No. 3 (12 February 1986): 4ff.

Provides interesting and useful comments and statistics on the Oscar nominations for 1985.

413. McDowell, Edwin. "Writers Union Meeting Criticizes Publishers." New York Times, Section C (22 October 1984): 19.
Discusses Walker's participation in a week-end conference on Censorship and Culture. Criticizes corporate America for its domination of the book publishing industry and the media, as well as erosion in the royalty rate paid to authors.

414. Nolan, Lani M. "On 'Anais Nin: 1903-1977'." Ms. 6, No. 2 (August 1977): 7-8.
Criticizes Walker for her portrayal of Nin and argues that Nin's works have earned her the title of "visionary." (See Walker's reply to Nolan in the listings of "Essays and Letters.")

415. O'Leary, Donald J. "On The Diary of An African Nun." Freedomways 9, No. 1 (First Quarter 1969): 70-71.
Objects to Walker's "violent attack on virginity undertaken for the love of God and mankind." (See Walker's reply to O'Leary in the listing of "Essays and Letters.")

416 Oliver, Stephanie Stokes. "Margaret 'Shug' Avery: Beyond

'The Color Purple'." Essence 17, No. 5 (September 1986): 118-120ff.
Spotlights Margaret Avery as she recalls the deprivations she suffered prior to landing her role in The Color Purple. Affirms faith in herself and points toward new directions in her career as an actress.

417. Rose, Pat. "Growing Books at Wild Trees Press." Small Press 4, No. 2 (November/December 1986): 30-35. Describes Walker's venture into the publishing industry, her commitment to a small press dedicated to helping new writers get started, and her insistence on publishing books about people who are capable of political change and who are "active in their own liberation."

Addendum

Burnett, Zaron W. "*The Color Purple*: Personal Reaction." *Catalyst*, premiere issue (Fall 1986): 43-44.

Contends that critics are unjustified in questioning Walker's portrayal of Black men because the characters in *The Color Purple* represent Walker's own unique experiences. Argues that the reader should accept Walker's art for its potentiality for enriching our lives.

Mullen, Harryette. "Daughters in Search of Mothers or a Girl Child in a Family of Men." *Catalyst*, premiere issue (Fall 1986): 45-49.

Rejects the arguments that *The Color Purple* attacks Black Men and proposes lesbianism as a panacea for Black Women who are brutalized and victimized by their men. Contends that Walker's intention is to condemn the prevailing system of patriarchy and suggest lesbianism as a possibility for facilitating the bonding of women and creating a radical alternative to the existing patriarchal structure.

Wade-Gales, Gloria. "Anatomy of An Error: *The Color Purple* Controversy." *Catalyst*, premiere issue (Fall 1986): 50-53.

Examines charges of negative Black male images, incest, and lesbianism which have been made against Walker's novel. Concludes that *The Color Purple* should be evaluated as fiction within a literary context and that social conditioning by whites has frequently prevented Blacks from making an objective assessment of the work.

About the Authors

Louis H. Pratt is Professor of English and Chairman of the Department of Languages and Literature at Florida A and M University. A graduate of Savannah State College, he holds the M.A. and Ph.D. degrees, respectively, from Teachers College, Columbia University, and Florida State University. Dr. Pratt is the author of _James Baldwin_ (G. K. Hall and Company, 1978). He has contributed articles to the _Critical Survey of Short Fiction_ (Salem Press, 1981), _Dictionary of Black Theatre_ Greenwood Press, 1983), _Critical Survey of Long Fiction_ (Salem Press, 1983), and _Critical Essays on James Baldwin_ (G. K. Hall and Company, forthcoming publication). His dissertation, "The Mystery of the Human Being: A Critical Study of the Writings of James Baldwin," was cited as "a major contribution to contemporary critical literature." As a result, Dr. Pratt received the first annual J. Russell Reaver Award at Florida State University for the best creative scholarship in American literature or folklore. Dr. Pratt has presented papers at the College Language Association, the Popular Culture Association of America, the Middle Atlantic Writers Association, the Modern Language Association, and the South Atlantic Modern Language Association.

Darnell D. Pratt is Head of Acquisitions at the State Library of Florida and a former President of the Alumni Board of

Directors of the School of Library and Information Studies, Florida State University. A former teacher and secretary, Mrs. Pratt received the B.S. degree from Savannah State College and the M.S. degree from Florida State University. Currently, she is enrolled in the Florida Certified Public Managers Program, and she served as the affiliate representative for the Florida Library Association to the American Library Association, Junior Members Roundtable, for 1985-86. Mrs. Pratt is co-author (a-long with Dr. Pratt) of a bio-bibliography on novelist Toni Morrison which is in progress and currently under contract with Greeenwood Press.

Index

(Numbers refer to items; numbers in parentheses refer to pages.)

A

C

D

Y

Z